KV-190-493

THE NEW
FREEZER
COOKBOOK

THE NEW
FREEZER
COOKBOOK

MARY NORWAK

WARD LOCK LIMITED · LONDON

© Mary Norwak   1985

First published in Great Britain in 1985
by Ward Lock Limited, 82 Gower Street,
London WC1E 6EQ, an Egmont Company.

All Rights Reserved. No part of this publication
may be reproduced, stored in a retrieval system,
or transmitted, in any form or by any means,
electronic, mechanical, photocopying, recording,
or otherwise, without the prior permission of the
Copyright owners.

Designed by Melissa Orrom
Text filmset in Bembo
by Paul Hicks Limited, Plymouth

Printed and bound in Spain by
Graficromo S.A., Cordoba

**British Library Cataloguing in Publication
Data**

Norwak, Mary
    The new freezer cookbook.
    1. Home freezers – Amateurs' manuals
    I. Title
    641.4′53   TX610

ISBN 0-7063-6406-6

CONTENTS

Notes

It is important to follow *either* the metric *or* the imperial measures when using the recipes in this book. Do not use a combination of measures.

Each recipe will serve 4–6 people, according to appetite.

Acknowledgements

The author and publishers would like to thank the following organizations and companies for their help with the photographs in this book:

Brazilian Fruit and Vegetable Information Bureau (page 47); British Meat (pages 83 and 87); Colmans of Norwich (pages 63 and 67); Duck Information Service (page 79); Electricity Council (page 11); Gales Honey Bureau (page 59); Heritage Housewares (page 26); RHM Foods Ltd (pages 23, 107, 126 and 127); Stork Cookery Service (pages 95 and 130–31); Tate and Lyle Refineries (pages 118 and 139); Thorn EMI Major Domestic Appliances Ltd (pages 10 and 11); Thorpac Group plc (page 22).

INTRODUCTION

An efficient home-freezing system can save money through economic purchasing of seasonal or commercially frozen raw materials, but it can also save considerable shopping and food preparation time by means of bulk buying and batch cooking. It can also enable different members of a family to heat and eat dishes at their convenience, rather than relying on unhealthy snacks and expensive grills.

The well-run freezer can serve a dual purpose, combining the long-term storage of bulk raw materials from garden, farm, market or supermarket, and commercially frozen foods from freezer food centres, with the short-term storage of cooked dishes and leftovers which are meant to be used up quickly.

An extra dimension has been added to home freezing by the use of the microwave cooker. Not only can frozen food be very quickly reheated, but defrosting can be speeded up so much that frozen food becomes truly convenient.

This book combines the basic knowledge needed to buy this major kitchen appliance with useful information on the selection of raw materials, packaging and basic preparation to maintain food with a perfect texture, flavour and content. Additionally, there is a section on combining freezer and microwave techniques. The recipes, with specific information on how to freeze each one, are easy-to-follow and will prove useful for everyday meals and for special occasions.

Choosing a Freezer

A food freezer is a major appliance, and many factors must be considered when making a choice. Do not make decisions in a hurry, but compare types and prices, and assess the space available, the amount and type of food a family consumes, and whether there is a lot of entertaining, or a number of people at home all day.

TYPES OF FREEZER

THE CHEST FREEZER

This is particularly useful for placing in a garage or outhouse. It is excellent for bulk storage, but should be fitted with dividers and baskets to make organization easier. A short or fat person may have difficulty in using a chest cabinet, and may find baskets heavy and awkward to lift. See that a chest freezer has a self-balancing lid and a magnetic lid seal.

Most chest freezers have a fast-freezing compartment, divided from the cabinet by a panel. The fast-freezing switch cuts out thermostatic control so that the motor runs continuously. Heat is removed from the fresh food as quickly as possible, and already-stored foods do not rise in temperature. Sometimes the fast-freezing switch is connected to a light which will show when the motor is running continuously and the fast-freezing compartment is in action.

If there is no fast-freeze compartment, food can be frozen against the back, sides or base of the freezer, since these are the coldest parts of the cabinet.

THE UPRIGHT FREEZER

This type of freezer is generally more attractive in a kitchen, and has the advantage of easy access and quicker checks on food supplies. Upright freezers have their weight concentrated in a small area, and it is wise to see that floors will take this weight. It used to be said that there was a greater loss of cold air from the opening of an upright rather than a chest freezer, but this is in fact negligible. Look for high capacity shelves in doors and a good door seal. Check whether a short person can reach the back of upper shelves easily. Look for useful extras like interior lights and warning systems, and for special freezer shelves for fast freezing. Some models can be purchased which are entirely frost-free, ie they do not need to be defrosted.

REFRIGERATOR-FREEZER

Specially designed kitchens and small areas can be fitted with combination refrigerator-freezers.

Very popular are the half-and-half models, with equal-sized refrigerator and freezer; the refrigerator is often above the freezer, making for easier use.

Sometimes a small freezer is fitted on top of a large refrigerator; this is most suitable for freezing small packages.

FREEZER ACCESSORIES

Baskets can be used which hang across a cabinet freezer and slide along the top. Baskets can also be used on the floor of the cabinet; they are, however, heavy to lift when full.

Bags of brightly coloured nylon mesh used for shopping are useful for the floor of the freezer cabinet. They can be filled with bag-wrapped food and are easy to lift.

Polythene Bags in bright colours, and of a large size like laundry bags are also useful for holding a number of small items in a chest freezer. Use the colours for easy identification.

Dividers are useful in the bottom of chest freezers where heavy items are stored. These provide a useful and easily moved division to separate meat, fruit, vegetables and fish.

WHAT SIZE SHOULD YOU CHOOSE?

Many cabinets have particularly thin walls so that there is a greater storage capacity for their size. It is generally recommended that 56.5 litres/2 cubic feet capacity should be allowed for food for each member of the family, with 56.5 litres/2 cubic feet additional space (ie a three-person family should buy a 226.0 litres/8 cubic feet cabinet). In practice, this recommended size is rather low if full advantage is to be taken of buying bulky items like meat, or of using the garden or oven to capacity. A larger size may also be required if a number of members of the family work.

WHAT DOES A FREEZER COST TO RUN?

Running costs are, of course, affected by the size of the freezer cabinet and its design. They will also be affected by the warmth of the room in which the freezer stands, the number of times the cabinet is opened daily, and the length of time it is kept open. The amount of fresh food being frozen can also affect running costs and the temperature of the food when it is put inside the freezer. It is more economical to run a well-packed freezer as the packages provide insulation.

Running costs are also affected by basic electricity charges. As a rough guide, a 170 litre/6 cubic feet freezer uses .3kW per 28.3 litres/cubic foot per 24 hours. 339.5 litres/12 cubic feet uses .25kW per 28.3 litres/cubic foot in the same time; 510 litres/18 cubic feet uses .2kW per 28.3 litres/cubic foot in the same time.

SERVICE AGREEMENTS

Some suppliers offer a service agreement with their freezer; this involves an annual payment. If you do decide to sign a service agreement, make sure exactly what is covered, as it is possible the fee may only cover the cost of labour and not the spare parts or vice versa.

Left: Half and half refrigerator freezers often have the refrigerator above the freezer, making for easier use

Right: A large refrigerator fitted with a small freezer is best suited to freezing small packages

Left: Upright freezers have their weight concentrated in a small area

Below: A chest freezer should be fitted with baskets and dividers to make organization easier

INSTALLING AND MAINTAINING THE FREEZER

You have chosen your freezer and arranged the day of delivery. See that somebody is at home to supervize the installation of the freezer, as it is important that it is positioned correctly.

Here are some guidelines to help you to choose the site which provides maximum efficiency and economical running.

1   Choose a dry, cool and airy place.
2   Avoid a damp place, an unventilated cupboard, direct sunlight (eg a sun room), excessive warmth (eg next to a cooker, boiler or radiator).
3   Choose the cool part of the kitchen, a large airy larder, a dry garage or outhouse, a utility room, spare room or passage.
4   Put the freezer near a table, and near good natural or artificial light, for ease of packing and unpacking.
5   Put it in a position away from a wall.
6   Raise it on wooden blocks or bricks if locating it in a garage or outhouse so that there is an airspace beneath.

PREPARING THE FREEZER FOR USE

The installation engineer will probably set the controls for you and switch on the power to see that the freezer motor is running correctly. It is, however, inadvisable to start using the freezer immediately. Follow these procedures first:

1   Check with the manufacturer's booklet that the controls have been correctly set by the supplier and tested.
2   Wash the inside of the freezer with plain water, and dry thoroughly.
3   Switch on the freezer and leave it for 12 hours before filling so that the cabinet is thoroughly chilled.
4   Set the control knob to the recommended temperature for everyday use.
5   Cover the plug and switch with a strip of adhesive tape. This will prevent children switching off the supply, and the casual unintentional use of the same socket for other domestic appliances.

DEFROSTING

Most freezers require defrosting. This should be carried out once or twice a year when frost is about 6mm/¼ inch thick and food stocks are low.

BEFORE DEFROSTING

Put on fast-freeze switch the day before defrosting so that food packages are very cold. If there is no fast-freeze compartment, turn down the freezer to its coldest temperature.

DURING DEFROSTING

1   Take out food packages, wrap them in cold newspaper and/or blankets, and keep in a cold place.
2   Turn off freezer, and disconnect from electricity supply.
3   Put newspapers or towels on the floor of the freezer.
4   Scrape down frost with a plastic or wooden spatula. *Do not use sharp tools or wire brushes.*
5   Cold water can be used to speed melting ice. *Do not use hot water, heaters or lamps.*
6   Leave cabinet open, and mop up moisture with clean cloths.

AFTER DEFROSTING

1   Wash the cabinet inside with warm water and a little bicarbonate of soda (15ml/1 tablespoon soda to 1.2 litres/2 pints water).
2   Rinse with clean water and dry thoroughly. *Do not use soap, detergent or caustic cleaners.*
3   Switch control to coldest setting, and run the freezer for 30 minutes.
4   Repack the freezer, checking packages for damage. Arrange items to be used up quickly at the top or front.
5   After 3 hours, return control to normal setting.

DO NOT FREEZE ANY FRESH FOOD FOR 24 HOURS AFTER DEFROSTING.

CLEANING THE EXTERIOR

Keep the freezer covered with a thick sheet of polythene to protect the cabinet if it is in an outside building. Wash the outside occasionally with warm soapy water, and polish with an enamel surface polish.

GOING ON HOLIDAY

Leave the freezer switched on during short holidays, and stock up with useful items like bread and cooked dishes. During a long break away from home, with the mains switch turned off, empty and clean out the freezer, and leave the lid or door open.

MOVING HOUSE

For a one-day move, run down the food stocks as low as possible. Put on the fast-freeze switch 24 hours beforehand so that the food is very cold. See that the removal firm will handle the cabinet and contents, and that they will load the freezer last and unload it first. Check that a socket is ready to receive the freezer at once, and that the electricity supply is switched on. If the move will take a long time, use up the food stock, and clean the cabinet before transferring it to the new home.

Note If a freezer is empty and open, it can be a danger to children who may climb inside and shut the door or lid without being able to open it again. It is important that such a freezer should be stored in a locked room or garage and the key removed.

WHEN THINGS GO WRONG

The worst thing that can happen to a freezer full of food is a power failure – or, you may suddenly notice that the freezer motor has not started up for some time. Here is an action checklist to cope with the situation.

1   Check if the switch has been turned off by mistake.
2   Check the fuses.
3   Check if the power failure is general and if the Electricity Board has been informed.
4   Do not touch the freezer motor.
5   Do not open the lid or door.
6   Leave the door or lid closed for 2 hours after supply is restored.
7   When power is restored, check the condition of food. It should last in good condition for 24 hours if the cabinet is well-insulated and full of food.
8   Quickly use up food which has thawed. Meat, fruit, pastry and vegetables may be cooked for re-freezing.

Note If your electricity supply and fuses are in order, call your freezer maintenance service immediately.

INSURING THE FREEZER

An insurance policy will cover the food in the freezer against various kinds of loss, but not against the accidental switching off of the machine, nor against the failure of power through industrial action. *Read the conditions of the policy carefully.* Such a policy is invaluable as it ensures against the loss of money spent on raw materials, packaging and time spent in preparation.

Buying Food in Bulk

Most people assume that buying in bulk will lead to a considerable saving in the family budget. Savings depend, however, on the number of people in the family, on shopping and eating habits and the accessibility of shops. Freezer owners find, in fact, that they save on such hidden factors as public transport fares, or petrol and parking charges for cars, and also on a great deal of shopping time (which represents money). They also find that, despite their overall shopping bills often remaining the same, they tend to live better, since the price of better cuts of meat or out-of-season vegetables is balanced by freezing cheaper meat or home produce.

HOW TO BUY IN BULK

Before making out bulk orders, check how the family money is spent and where the greatest savings can be made. Keep a month's or year's budget in mind, and see if more money can be saved by freezing slow-cooked dishes of economy cuts of meat, by home-baking bread and cakes, or by growing fruit and vegetables. See what proportion of each type of food will save money if stored in the freezer, or will save time if more important.

See that bulk food is properly packed for long-term storage. Food originally prepared for commercial and rapid use may come simply packed in cardboard boxes or a polythene bag. A 3.2kg/7 lb slab of pastry or 4.5kg/10 lb minced meat clinging together in an enormous lump will be almost useless under home conditions. Be prepared to re-pack large purchases in usable quantities as soon as the food is purchased. Check also whether it will be more convenient and cheaper in the long run to buy a bulk quantity of individual or family-size portions rather than enormous packs which are difficult to handle and store.

Some consideration must also be given to high quality storage life. There is little point in buying a large pack of fish fingers for instance, if the family cannot eat these up in 3 months, as quality, flavour and texture deteriorate when the storage life is exceeded.

WHERE TO BUY IN BULK
DELIVERY SERVICES

Some frozen food manufacturers and freezer centres deliver in bulk to the door. This is a most convenient way of ordering food since it can be transferred straight from the refrigerated van to the freezer, and it is particularly useful in country areas. A minimum order is normally stipulated, and it is worth preparing a bulk order with friends to make the delivery a worth-while business.

FROZEN FOOD CENTRES

These are found in many towns, and are useful for buying a wide variety of foods in both family and commercial pack sizes. They are useful places for trying new items before placing bulk orders, and the customer has the advantage of seeing and comparing the types of food. Try to choose a centre from which food can be taken home quickly, or which is near a good parking space.

SPECIALIST PRODUCERS

Meat, in particular, is sold by specialist producers, either frozen or prepared for freezing. Such firms operate delivery services or express postal services, or food can be collected. The quality is usually high.

LOCAL SHOPS, MARKETS AND FARMS

Local shops, markets and growers can usually supply fruit by the case and vegetables by the sack at reduced rates. A check should be kept on quality, as food may remain in the shops for some days before sale. It is not a good idea to buy in this way if time is short, as there is a lot of labour involved in preparing a sack of vegetables for the freezer. Farmers often supply vegetables, fruit, meat or poultry, and fruit or vegetables are often very cheap if picked by the customer. Fish and shellfish are worth buying direct from the boat or from a seaside shop which has daily supplies.

GETTING BULK-BUYS HOME

It is important to insulate frozen food well after purchasing. Pack tightly in an insulated bag to obtain maximum value.

Ready-made insulated bags are available, but these can be improvized by the use of newspapers or blankets.

If buying frozen food in a supermarket or other general store, pack the frozen food last so that it can be unpacked and stored first.

WHAT TO BUY IN BULK

BREAD AND CAKES

Considerable time is saved by buying baked goods in bulk, eg crusty loaves, bread made from special flours, rolls and baps, sliced loaves for sandwiches and toast, buns, crumpets, malt and fruit loaves and cakes.

CONVENIENCE FOODS

Food which has been prepared to save cooking and serving time is useful for quick meals, and particularly for in-between meals such as high tea for children. There are considerable savings in bulk packs of hamburgers, fish fingers, fish cakes, sausages and thin cuts of meat and fish. Check the different kinds of variations in flavour and texture to see which are most popular with the family.

PREPARED DISHES

Prepared dishes, casseroles, puddings and gourmet dishes are useful for families with little time for cooking. They should be bought in sizes most convenient for family use or for entertaining. Party dishes which need elaborate ingredients or lengthy cooking time are also useful. It is a good idea to buy small sizes first to see if they are acceptable.

FRUIT AND VEGETABLES

As farm and market produce take time for preparation, it may be more useful to buy commercially frozen fruit and vegetables in large packs. Particularly useful are such items as chips, mushrooms, green and red peppers, onions and mixed casserole vegetables. These are all in constant use in the kitchen, but are not always on hand in an accessible shop; nor are they particularly easy to prepare for freezing at home. Small quantities for recipe use can be shaken out of loose-packed commercial bags.

ICE CREAM

Ice cream in bulk containers is useful for a family with children. The quality soon deteriorates, however, if a container is frequently opened and 'scooped', and the product has a relatively short high quality life, so it may be more practical to buy bulk supplies of smaller packs, or of individual ices such as lollies and chocolate bars which are easy to serve and have a longer storage life.

POULTRY

Whole birds and poultry pieces are very useful for converting into cooked dishes for the freezer for both family use and entertaining. Some farms and shops prepare free-range birds in quantity for home freezing; others supply commercially frozen poultry in bulk.

It is best to pack giblets and livers separately in bulk for the freezer as they do not store well inside birds, and are useful on their own for many recipes.

MEAT

Meat is usually the most expensive item in the family budget, and is one of the most useful raw materials to buy in bulk. Bulk meat needs careful buying, and it is worth studying the problems before making an expensive purchase.

It is usually most practical to buy enough meat for the family's needs for 3 months, which is a reasonable turnover time and about the cheapest length of time to store the meat, allowing for the running costs of a freezer. It is a great mistake to purchase a quarter of beef, a pig and a lamb all at the same time since this overloads the freezer at the expense of other items. Pork, in particular, may deteriorate if kept beyond the recommended high quality storage life period. It is better to combine with one or two other families to get the advantage of bulk purchase with a variety of types of meat and different cuts.

Whole carcasses are ideal for those who will cook and eat cheaper cuts. Otherwise these will be wasted, and the roasting and grilling cuts will prove more expensive in the end. If a family only likes the better cuts, it is better to make a bulk purchase of these or to buy a good variety pack of different meats.

Beef is a really bulky purchase. A forequarter will account for about 45kg/100 lb and a hindquarter is even larger. The forequarter is more manageable, but consists mainly of slow-cooking cuts. Boned joints take up far less space in the freezer. The bones will account for about one-quarter of a bulk purchase, but can be made into concentrated stock for freezing (the butcher should be asked to saw them into reasonable pieces for the saucepan). Suet can be used for a wide variety of puddings, and can also be rendered down for fat. Check whether bones and suet are included in the overall price and if they will be delivered with the meat. Have the slow-cooking meat cut into slices and/or cubes for easy use, and ask for plenty of lean mince in 450g/ 1lb packs. Try to convert some of the cuts straight into pies or casseroles when they are delivered; this will save freezer space and provide some useful meals for quick use.

Veal is not very often available in bulk, and is not very successful in the freezer, since it tends to lose flavour in storage conditions. If veal is bought, see that it is carefully divided into prepared boned roasting joints, escalopes and chops, and pie veal, etc.

Lamb is worth buying. A small lean one will weigh 11.25kg–13.5kg/25–30 lb with little waste. Decide if you want chops in roasting joints or divided. If the cheaper chops and breast of lamb are not liked, it may be better value to buy roasting joints and bags of chops.

Pork has a shorter storage life than other meats and should not be purchased in over-large quantities. Half a pig will weigh about 22.5kg/50 lb and consists mostly of roasting and frying joints. The head and trotters may be included, but freezer space should not be wasted on them. They are better used at once in brawn or a dish which requires meat jelly.

COOKING AND PACKING FOR THE FREEZER

It can be all too easy to become a slave to the freezer, endlessly shopping and cooking to keep the box topped up. It is important to take advantage of the fact that this is the only way of safely preserving cooked dishes. Cooking should be organized ahead so that two or three ready meals are always 'in hand' in the freezer. The great thing is to avoid inflicting the same kind of food on the family for weeks ahead.

Before cooking foods for freezing, it is wise to assess which items are worth freezer space. Briefly, these are:

1   Dishes which need long cooking or long and tedious preparation
2   Dishes made from seasonal foods
3   Dishes which can be made in large quantities with little more work (ie three cakes instead of one; double or treble casseroles)
4   Dishes for special occasions, such as parties or holidays
5   Convenience foods for invalids, small children, etc.

FOODS TO FREEZE WITH CARE

Onions, garlic, spices and herbs. They sometimes get a musty flavour in cooked dishes in the freezer, and quantities should be reduced in such dishes as casseroles, and adjusted during reheating. Careful packing will help to prevent these strong flavours spreading to other food, and a short storage life is recommended.

Rice, spaghetti and potatoes should only be frozen without liquid. They become mushy in liquid and should not be frozen in soups or stews.

Sauces and gravy are best thickened by reduction, or with tomato or vegetable purée. If flour is used, it must be reheated with great care, preferably in a double saucepan, to avoid separation. Cornflour can be used but gives a glutinous quality. Egg and cream thickening should be added after freezing.

Bananas, apples, pears, whole melons, and avocados cannot be successfully frozen whole to eat raw. They can be prepared in various ways for freezer storage (although pears are never very satisfactory). Bananas are not worthwhile as they are in season at a reasonable price throughout the year.

Cabbage cannot be frozen successfully to eat raw, and is not worth freezing as it occupies valuable freezer space. Red cabbage may be useful to keep frozen, as it has a short season and is never very plentiful.

Celery and chicory cannot be frozen to eat raw. They are useful to freeze in liquid to serve as vegetables. Celery can be used in stews or soup.

Tomatoes cannot be frozen to eat raw, but are invaluable for soups, stews and sauces, or to freeze as purée or juice.

Milk must be homogenized and packed in waxed cartons.

FOODS TO AVOID FREEZING

Nearly all foods freeze well, but there are a few items to avoid completely, or to freeze only with great care. A few other foods cannot be frozen to eat raw, but can be used for cooking.

Foods unsuitable for freezing:

Hard-boiled eggs (including Scotch eggs, eggs in pies and in sandwiches)

Soured cream and single cream (less than 40% butterfat) which separate

Custards (including tarts). The custard mixture of eggs and milk can be frozen uncooked but there is little point in this.

Soft meringue toppings

Mayonnaise and salad dressings

Milk puddings

Royal icing and frosting without fat

Salad vegetables with a high water content, eg lettuce, watercress

Old boiled potatoes (potatoes can be frozen mashed, roasted, baked or as chips)

Stuffed poultry (the storage life of stuffing is very short)

Food with a high proportion of gelatine

Whole eggs in shells which will crack

CHOOSING THE RIGHT PACKAGING

Packaging is important to retain the quality of frozen food. Buy the minimum necessary to begin with, but see that it is of good quality, and do not waste the money spent on good food by using inferior packaging.

On the other hand, it is not necessary to spend a lot of money on sophisticated or complicated packaging methods. Try the basic essentials first. Most people find they manage with a combination of rigid containers, polythene bags and sheet foil, but the choice will depend a great deal on the type of food most commonly packed, and how important it is to save freezer space by using easily stacked containers. The important thing to remember is that the aim of packaging is to eliminate air at the beginning of the freezing process, and to exclude air during storage.

If air penetrates the food, moisture leaves it. Food must also be protected from cross-contamination of flavours and smells, and delicate foods must be protected from bruising or chipping.

Packaging for freezing foods is specially marked and can be found in a variety of shops and stores. Check the following points before choosing packaging for a specific food.

1 See that packaging does not allow air or moisture to penetrate (this is known as moisture-vapour-proof packaging).
2 Check that packaging is waterproof and cannot leak.
3 See that packaging is greaseproof, thereby avoiding rancid smells. These can also be caused by poorly cleaned or stored packaging, and by some materials which smell strongly.
4 Check that packaging is resistant to low temperatures for a long time. Some plastics become brittle, split and crack. Glass jars must also be tested before use (see page 24).

RIGID CONTAINERS

Plastic boxes with close-fitting lids can be used indefinitely, and are extremely useful for frozen items such as sandwiches for lunches which may be carried while thawing. They are also useful for items like stews which can be turned out into a saucepan for thawing, as the flexible sides can be lightly pressed to aid removal. For long-term storage, it is important that the boxes have perfectly fitting airtight lids. Choose square or rectangular containers which stack easily.

FOIL

Foil is an invaluable freezer packaging as it is clean, easy to handle, and, with care, can be re-used a number of times.

Sheet foil is specially made for freezer use and is good for wrapping awkward parcels as it can be moulded close to the food. It can also be used to make lids for other containers. Ordinary household foil can be used, but two thicknesses give the best protection.

Foil dishes, pie plates and pudding basins are useful for cooking food which can then be frozen in the same container, followed by reheating. These containers can be covered with a lid of sheet foil, or they can be packed in polythene sheeting or polythene bags.

Deep foil dishes are obtainable with specially treated cardboard lids to protect the food. These are useful for casseroles, cottage pies, meat balls in gravy, meat and poultry slices in gravy, and a variety of sweet puddings. The food can be prepared in the containers, then covered with the lids on which the name of the food can be written. The containers can be re-used, but the lids are rarely usable a second time and can be replaced by sheet foil.

Gusseted bags made from foil or foil-paper laminate, are easy to fill and store, and are particularly suitable for such items as cheese since they prevent cross-contamination of smells.

POLYTHENE SHEETS

These sheets are useful for wrapping joints, poultry and large pies, and pieces of sheeting may be used to divide meat, etc, for easy thawing. The wrapping must be sealed with special freezer tape.

POLYTHENE BAGS

These bags are very cheap to use and simple to handle. They should be strong and of a heavy gauge designed for the freezer. They may be used for meat, poultry, fruit and vegetables, pies, cakes and sandwiches. Buy bags which are gusseted for easy packing. They may be sealed by heat or twist fastening. If the bags are subjected to frequent handling, they should be overwrapped to avoid punctures. If the contents are likely to contaminate other items with their smell and flavour, they should also be overwrapped. Coloured bags aid identification in the freezer.

Consider the alternatives given in the chart on page 23 if some types of packaging are not easily available.

Rigid containers should have perfectly fitting airtight lids

Item	Rigid Containers	Foil Containers	Foil Sheeting	Polythene Bags or Sheeting
Fresh Meat			★	★
Fresh Poultry and Game			★	★
Fresh Fish			★	★
Cooked Meat and Fish Dishes	★	★	★	★
Fresh Vegetables	★			★
Fresh Fruit (unsweetened or dry sugar pack)	★			★
Fresh Fruit (syrup pack)	★			
Cheese			★	★
Eggs	★			
Soups and Sauces	★			
Bread, Cakes and Biscuits			★	★
Pastry and Pies		★	★	★
Puddings	★	★	★	★
Ice Cream	★			

A selection of packaging equipment

SUBSTITUTE PACKAGING

Whereas specially bought packing has been tested under freezer conditions, substitute packaging must be tested in a freezer before use as many everyday materials are not suitable.

Packages from commercially frozen food, ice cream containers, and some grocery packs (eg cottage cheese cartons, margarine tubs) can be used for home freezing after being cleaned and tested.

Screw top preserving jars, bottles and honey jars may also be used after being tested for resistance to low temperatures. To do this, put an empty jar into a plastic bag and put into the freezer overnight; if the jar breaks, the bag will hold the pieces.

Remember to allow 1–2.5cm/½–1 inch headspace for expansion which might otherwise cause breakage.

FASTENING MATERIALS

All packages must be sealed by one of three methods:

Taping   Special freezer-proof tape must be used for sealing wrapped packages and on containers with lids.

Heat   Polythene bags may be sealed by a heat sealing unit – this is a machine for welding polythene – or by a domestic iron. Put a piece of paper between the iron and the polythene to be fused, and iron over this.

Twist-tying   After extracting air from a polythene bag, a plastic-covered fastener should be twisted round the end of the bag, the top of the bag turned down over this twist and the fastener twisted again round the bunched neck of the bag.

LABELLING MATERIALS

All items in a freezer should be clearly labelled with contents, weight or number of portions, date of freezing, and any special thawing, heating or seasoning instructions.

Special labels are made for freezer use, with gum which is resistant to low temperatures. Ordinary gummed labels will curl and drop off at low temperatures, while tie-on labels may tear off during storage. Twist-ties with attached labels are available. In transparent packages, ordinary paper labels may be placed *inside* the pack, but they may be difficult to read if frosting occurs. Alternatively, write directly on the freezer wrap. Labels must be written in wax crayon, felt pen or Chinagraph pencil; ordinary ink is not suitable as it fades.

Colour Identification

Coloured lids, labels and bags are available in a wide range of colours to suit every need. A colour can be used to identify one type of food (eg red tops for fruit containers), or to sub-divide a food category (eg red for raspberries; green for gooseberries). Large coloured bags can be used for collecting together all items in one food category. Coloured labels are the quickest and cheapest aid to identification.

Recording

Record the type of food frozen, the number and size of packages, and the date of freezing for all items in the freezer. Use an exercise book, log book or freezer diary. The length of high quality storage life should be noted if possible, and it is a good idea to note how many packages have been removed. Some people also like to record the position occupied in the freezer, but this may be difficult to maintain.

CONTENTS	NO. AND SIZE OF PACKAGES	DATE OF FREEZING	STORAGE LIFE	USED
Gooseberries	4 × 450g/1 lb	Aug 1985	12 months	11
Minced beef	3 × 900g/2 lb	Aug 1985	2 months	1

FREEZING FOR THE MICROWAVE

The shape of microwave containers is important for best results. A round container will allow more even cooking, while an oval one allows food to cook more quickly at the narrow ends. Shallow dishes allow heat to spread more evenly through the food. A straight-sided container allows the microwave to penetrate more evenly than one with curved sides.

Ovenglass and ovenware may be used both for freezing and microwaving as long as there is no metallic decoration on the dish – this causes arcing in the cooker. Boil-in-bags are useful for semi-liquid items and for vegetables, and these may be used if the closing tags are replaced by string. Disposable freezer/microwave dishes are also useful. Most importantly, foil dishes must *not* be used for microwaving, and it is best to substitute special freezer/microwave ware.

Freezer-to-microwave ware is a mixture of polythene and polystyrene materials, and may be re-used many times. The containers should not be used for high-fat or high-sugar food as the high temperature of the contents will melt the dishes. They cannot be used in conventional ovens, but prepared dishes may be placed in them, or a dish may be cooked in the microwave cooker, frozen in the same dish, and then reheated in it. This type of cookware should be overwrapped in a polythene bag for freezing.

Ovenable board is a good substitute for foil, and is made from polyester-coated paperboard which can be used in the freezer, microwave cooker and a conventional oven up to a temperature of 200°C/400°F/Gas 6. The dishes are rigid and may be used on a table.

Continuous usage microwave ovenware looks like ceramic and is non-flammable. The dishes may be used in a conventional oven up to a temperature of 200°C/400°F/Gas 6, in a freezer and in a microwave cooker.

25

A selection of microwave cookware which can be used straight from the freezer

PACKAGING TECHNIQUES

Before beginning the freezing process, collect together all the packaging materials including sealing equipment and labels. The freezer is easier to organize if food is packed in neat shapes. Square or rectangular containers are easier to pack than cylindrical ones or tubs. Bags can be formed into square shapes during freezing (see page 29). Awkward packages such as joints of meat are best collected together in baskets or large bags. Fragile cakes and pies are best packed in rigid square containers or cake boxes.

To exclude air and remove air pockets in packages, press the package with the hands, by sucking out air with a straw or special pump, or by exerting water pressure on the package placed in a bowl of water. Air pockets in rigid containers can be released by plunging a knife into the contents two or three times.

SHEET WRAPPING

Foil or polythene sheeting can be used for wrapping. This can be used in two ways.

Chemist's Wrap   Put the food in the centre of the sheet of wrapping material. Bring the two sides of the sheet together above the food and fold them neatly downwards over the food. Bring the wrapping as close to the food as possible, pressing out the air. Seal the fold of the wrapping, then fold the ends in like a parcel, making them close and tight and excluding air. Seal all folds.

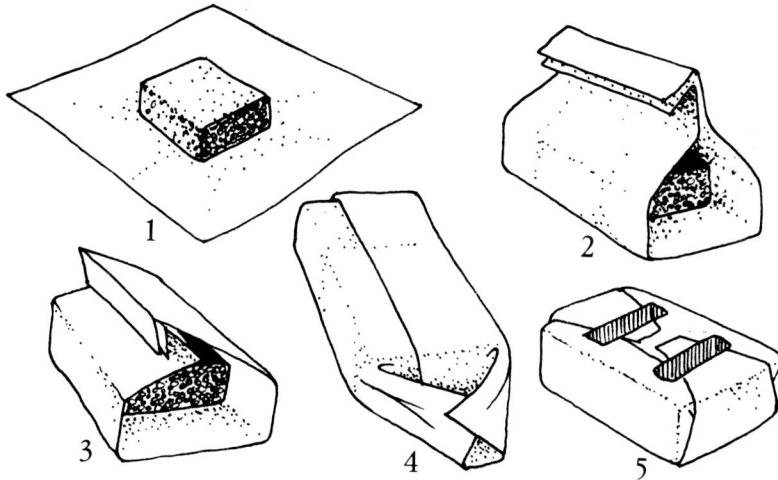

Butcher's Wrap Put the food diagonally on the sheet of wrapping material. Bring in the opposite corners and seal them. Bring in a third corner and then fold over the last corner. Seal all openings. This pack is slightly less bulky than the chemist's wrap, and is more easily used for slightly irregular packages such as bone-in meat.

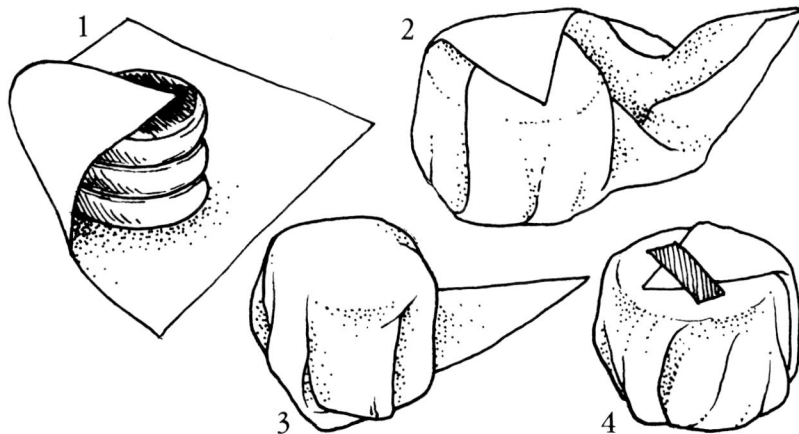

CONTAINER PACKING

Moisture will expand during freezing, so headspace must be left between the surface of the food and the seal of the container. This is usually 2.5cm/1 inch space above the food, but if containers are narrow, allow 1.5–2.5cm/¾–1 inch headspace.

1   Fill containers carefully to avoid soiling the rims if liquid food is being packed. Use a funnel or scoop to aid packing.
2   Leave headspace above the food. Fruit packed in syrup will rise to the surface

and discolour, so a crumpled piece of foil or transparent film should be placed into the headspace to weigh the food down.

3   Press on the container lid firmly. If it does not have a patent seal, finish with freezer tape.

BAG PACKING

1   Fill bags carefully, making sure food goes into the corners, and using a funnel or scoop to avoid soiling the edges of the bags. Put bags into sugar boxes, rigid containers or fruit punnets so that they freeze into a neat square shape.

2   Extract as much air as possible, and close the bag with a wire twist fastener. For extra security, bend the long end of the bag back into the wire twist, making a second turn of the fastener.

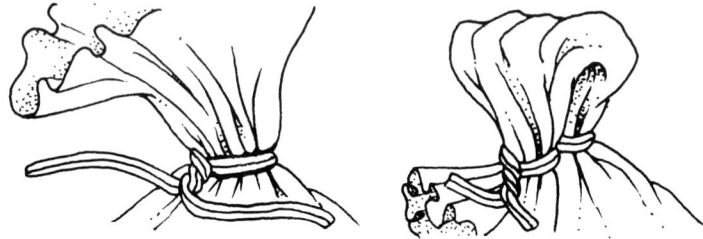

PADDING AND SEPARATING

Before packing small pieces of meat, fish or cake layers, separate them with foil, polythene or transparent film. Pad the bones of meat or poultry with twists of paper or foil.

OPEN FREEZING

Most food stored in a single pack will become solid when frozen. To keep small items of food separate, such as strawberries or peas, freeze them unwrapped on small trays, baking sheets or large lids from rigid containers. When the food is hard, pack in usable quantities in rigid containers or bags, sealed and labelled. This means that the food can be shaken out in small quantities from the pack, and it also helps to keep food such as strawberries in good shape.

Iced cakes and delicate pies are also best open frozen before packing so that they are not smudged or crushed. They can then be packed in crushproof boxes or in bags, or wrapped in foil.

CUBE AND BRICK FREEZING

Rigid containers need not be wasted on liquids. Small quantities of sauces, syrups, baby foods and herbs can be frozen in ice cube trays. When the cubes are frozen, they should be removed from the tray and placed in a polythene bag for storage. For easy separation, they can be wrapped in twists of foil or sprayed with soda water before packing in bags. One cube will be a useful portion for many recipes.

Larger quantities of liquid such as soup or purée can be frozen in brick shapes.

This is most easily done by pouring the liquid into a loaf tin or rigid container. When it has frozen into a solid 'brick', remove from the container, and wrap in foil or polythene for storage.

SHAPE FREEZING

Another way to save using expensive containers, is to freeze items in shaped foil or polythene in one of two ways:

1   Put a polythene bag into an empty sugar box. Fill with the food, eg fresh vegetables, fruit, liquids, seal the bag and freeze the food. After freezing, remove from the box and stack the neat square shapes. Empty fruit punnets can also be used to shape small square packages.
2   If a favourite casserole dish is needed over and over again and cannot be spared for the freezer, use it to shape the food which is going to be reheated in it. Line the dish with foil and pour in the recipe. Fold over the foil to make a package, and seal. After freezing, remove the package from the casserole and store it. When required, unwrap and return the shaped recipe to the casserole for heating and serving.
    Note Remember to test the casserole dish beforehand for resistance to freezing temperatures (see page 24).

ORGANIZING FREEZER SPACE

Arrange each type of food in date order so that items are not left in the freezer beyond their high quality storage life. Food to be used first must be most accessible.

Keep the food in use and do not use the freezer as a miser's hoard. Use it as a shop for supplying most of your daily needs and keep the 'stock' turning over, checking always on high quality storage life.

Have a basket or bag or shelf for all the odd items left from batches of food, eg the last iced cake, leftover stew, a spare pot of sauce, a few egg yolks, so that they are used up quickly.

Eliminate items which prove to be unpopular and do not waste next year's freezer space on them.

Upright freezers are easy to pack and keep tidy. Use the lowest shelf or compartment for meat and fish, and above this, have a compartment for vegetables and one for fruit. Vegetables and fruit can be combined on a shelf if space is limited, but will then need careful labelling or colour identification. Use upper shelves for convenience foods (eg fish fingers), and for cooked savoury dishes, cakes, puddings and desserts. These can be sub-divided if space is available, or combined but with identification. Door shelves are best used for short storage of small packs of sauces, dairy produce and pastry goods, and for single packs which are to be used up quickly. Label rigid containers on the *front*, and face labels forward so that they are quickly identified.

Chest freezers are less easy to organize, but have more space for bulk items. Use the bottom of the freezer for meat and fish, vegetables, and bulk ice cream containers in the proportion of space needed. Use baskets for fruit and for cooked dishes. Keep a basket, or part of one, for small packs of sauces, syrups, etc, and for food packages which are to be used quickly. The fast-freeze compartment may be used for storage, but should not contain frozen food when fresh food is being frozen down. Label containers on lids so that they can be chosen easily.

FREEZING CHECKLIST

1 Turn down the freezer to 'Coldest' or put on fast-freeze switch at least 2 hours before food will be ready to process.
2 Select packaging and equipment in various sizes, sealing and labelling equipment.
3 Prepare food quickly and cleanly.
4 Cool food *quickly*.
5 Open freeze fruit, vegetables and iced cakes if preferred.
6 Pack, seal and label carefully.
7 Arrange packs in coldest part of freezer or in fast-freeze compartment, avoiding a solid block of containers. (Do not add more than one-tenth of the entire freezer capacity at one time for freezing down, as this slows up the freezing process.)
8 While freezing is in progress, keep the packages away from other frozen food already in the cabinet.
9 Freeze packages till solid, remove to storage area, and re-adjust freezer temperature or fast-freeze switch to the 'normal storage' position.

IF THINGS GO WRONG

If food is correctly prepared for freezing, results should be good, and food should have a fine flavour and colour, and a good texture. Sometimes however, an item can prove disappointing, and it is worth checking what is wrong to prevent the problem recurring.

DEHYDRATION

Dehydration is the removal of moisture and juices from food, usually after a long period of storage. Meat is particularly subject to this problem, giving a tough, dry and tasteless result. It can only be avoided by careful wrapping in moisture-vapour-proof packaging.

OXIDATION

Oxidation is a process whereby oxygen moves inwards from air to food, so that food must be protected by the correct wrappings. Oxidation causes the mingling of oxygen with food fat cells, which react to form chemicals which give meat and fish a bad taste and smell, and fatty foods become rancid.

FREEZER BURN

Dehydration causes discoloured greyish-brown areas on the surface of food when it is removed from the freezer. It is only avoided by correct packaging materials, wrapping and sealing.

RANCIDITY

This is the effect of oxidation or absorption of oxygen into fat cells, and is recognized by the unpleasant flavour and smell of the food affected. Fried foods suffer from this problem, and are not generally recommended for freezer storage. Salt accelerates the reaction which causes rancidity and should not be added to minced meat or sausages before freezing; salt butter will have a shorter freezer life than fresh butter.

Pork is particularly subject to rancidity, since it contains not only thick layers of fat but also a greater number of tiny fat cells than other meat, so that its freezer life is shorter. Fat fish has similar problems.

CROSS-FLAVOURING

Strongly flavoured foods may affect other items in storage with their smell or flavour, and should be carefully overwrapped.

FLABBINESS

Fruit and vegetables which are flabby and limp may be of the wrong variety for freezing, or be overblanched. In general however, depending on cell structure, slow freezing of fruit and vegetables will result in flabbiness.

ICE CRYSTALS

Too great headspace on top of liquid foods such as soup may cause a layer of ice crystals to form which will affect storage and flavour. This is not too serious in liquids which will be heated or thawed, as the liquid melts back into its original form and can be shaken or stirred back into emulsion.

Meat, fish, vegetables and fruit can, however, be affected by ice crystals if slow freezing has taken place. Moisture in the food cells forms ice which will expand if slow-frozen, and, in occupying more space, these crystals will puncture and destroy surrounding tissues. This breaking down of tissues allows juices and flavour, particularly in meat, to escape. Fast freezing is essential for all foods.

FREEZING CHARTS

These are general guidelines only. Refer to the manufacturer's instructions if in doubt.

For information on defrosting and reheating in a microwave cooker, see page 57.

POULTRY AND GAME

Poultry should be starved for 24 hours before killing, then hung and bled well. Avoid skin damage when plucking. Cool birds in refrigerator for 12 hours, then draw and clean.

All game should be hung to its required state before freezing. Hanging after thawing will result in the flesh going bad.

Type	Preparation	Methods	High quality storage life	Thawing Instructions
Chicken, guinea fowl	Clean, truss whole bird, bone or joint.	Chill for 12 hours, then pack in polythene bag. Pack giblets separately. Do not stuff.	12 months	Thaw, unopened, overnight in refrigerator.
Duck, goose	Pluck while body is warm. Remove oil glands.	Chill well, then pack in polythene bag. Pack giblets separately. Do not stuff.	6 months	" "
Turkey	Clean, truss whole bird, bone or joint.	" "	12 months	Thaw in cold place, unopened, for 1½–3 days.
Grouse, pheasant, partridge	Remove shot, clean wounds, keep cool and hang to taste. Pluck, draw and truss.	Chill well, pad bones, pack in polythene bag.	6 months	Thaw, unopened, in refrigerator for 5 hours per 450g/ 1lb or 2 hours per 450g/ 1lb at room temperature.
Plover, quail, snipe, woodcock	Remove shot, clean wounds, pluck, truss (do not draw).	Chill well, pad bones, pack in polythene bag.	6 months	" "

Type	Preparation	Methods	High quality storage life	Thawing Instructions
Pigeon	Hang head downwards for 1 hour immediately after killing. Remove shot, clean wounds, pluck, draw and truss.	Chill well, then pack 2–3 together in polythene bag.	6 months	Thaw, unopened, in refrigerator for 5 hours per 450g/ 1lb or 2 hours per 450g/ 1lb at room temperature.
Hare	Choose animal with white teeth and fresh-looking fur. Clean shot wounds, behead and clean quickly, collecting blood if needed. Hang in cool place 1–12 days to taste. Skin, clean, joint.	Wrap joints separately, then pack together in polythene bag. Pack blood in separate carton.	6 months	,, ,,
Rabbit	Clean shot wounds, hang 24 hours in cool place, then skin, clean, joint.	Wrap joints separately, then pack together in polythene bag.	6 months	,, ,,
Venison	Clean wounds, keep carcass cold until butchered. Behead, skin, clean, wipe flesh dry. Hang for 4 days (up to 14 days in cold weather), joint.	Pack joints separately, then pack convenient quantities in polythene bags.	12 months	,, ,,
Giblets	Clean, wash, dry and chill.	Wrap in moisture-vapour-proof paper, or a bag, excluding air.	2 months	Thaw, unopened, in refrigerator for 2 hours.

MEAT

Both raw and cooked meat usually store extremely well in the freezer. It is, however, important to choose high-quality raw meat for storage, whether fresh or frozen, since freezing does not improve poor meat in either texture or flavour (although tender meat may become a little more tender in storage).

FAST FREEZING

Do not try to freeze more than 1.8kg/4 lb meat per 28.3 litres/cubic foot of freezer space, as meat must be frozen quickly. If there is a lot of meat to freeze, deal with offal first, then pork, veal and lamb, and finally beef. Keep the unfrozen meat in the refrigerator until it is ready to be processed. Fast freezing is essential to maintain the fine texture of the meat. If it is slow-frozen, it will coarsen, and will lose juices during thawing, resulting in loss of flavour and nutritive value.

Type	Preparation	Methods	High quality storage life	Thawing Instructions
Joints (beef, lamb, veal, pork)	Trim fat (bone if possible and roll), wipe meat.	Pad bones, pack in polythene bag or sheeting, or foil. Freeze quickly.	12 months (beef) 9 months (lamb and veal) 6 months (pork)	Thaw, unopened, overnight in refrigerator for 5 hours per 450g/1 lb, or for 2 hours at room temperature.
Joints (bacon)	Bacon is better if quick frozen, therefore cut pieces to not more than 2.3kg/5 lb.	Wrap in foil, put pack in clear polythene bag, then seal with tie.	8 weeks (smoked bacon) 5 weeks (unsmoked bacon)	Thaw slowly in refrigerator or at room temperature. Remove wrapping as soon as possible. Thaw vacuum-packed joints in bag, in refrigerator or at room temperature. Cook bacon immediately once it has thawed. Cooked bacon will keep for 1–2 days in refrigerator.
Steaks, chops, sliced meat	Trim fat, wipe meat.	Separate pieces with clingfilm or foil; pack in polythene bags.	6–12 months (according to meat)	Thaw in refrigerator, or cook from frozen in frying pan.
Cubed meat	—	Press tightly in bags or boxes. Freeze quickly.	2 months	Thaw in refrigerator for 3 hours, or cook from frozen.
Minced meat	Do not add salt. Shape into patties, if required.	Press tightly into bags or boxes. Separate patties with clingfilm; pack into bags or boxes.	2 months	Thaw, unopened, for 1½ hours at room temperature, or for 3 hours in refrigerator.

Type	Preparation	Methods	High quality storage life	Thawing Instructions
Hearts, kidneys, sweetbreads, tongue	Wash, dry well. Remove blood vessels and pipes.	Pack with care. Wrap in clingfilm or polythene, then pack in bags or boxes.	2 months	Thaw, unopened, for 1½ hours at room temperature, or for 3 hours in refrigerator.
Liver	Leave whole, or slice.	Separate slices with clingfilm; pack in polythene bags or sheeting.	2 months	,, ,,
Sausages, sausage-meat	Omit salt when preparing.	Pack in small quantities in bags. Overwrap tightly in polythene or foil.	1 month	,, ,,
Tripe	Cut into 2.5cm/1 inch squares.	Pack tightly into bags or boxes; freeze quickly.	2 months	Thaw unopened.
Galantines, meat loaf	a) Prepare in loaf tins lined with foil. b) Freeze in slices.	a) Fold foil over meat, then freeze and remove from tin in foil. b) Pack slices with clingfilm separators, pack in polythene for freezing.	2 months	Thaw quickly on absorbent paper.
Rashers, chops, steaks (bacon)		a) Wrap fresh-cut in polythene, then in foil. b) Wrap vacuum-packs in foil.	2–4 weeks	Thaw overnight in refrigerator. Bacon can be dipped in hot water until soft, then dried in paper towels before cooking. Cook immediately.

FISH AND SHELLFISH

If you intend to freeze fish at home, ensure that the fish is absolutely fresh and that you have the proper facilities for freezing and storage. Unless you can obtain really fresh supplies, it is better to rely on commercially frozen fish which has been processed with special equipment at very low temperatures.

Note Do not freeze fish in a domestic refrigerator, even one with a three-star compartment. Do not freeze fish in a conservator with a fixed temperature of around zero. This is intended for storage of commercially frozen produce only.

FRESHNESS IS PARAMOUNT

It is essential to know the history of the fish you plan to freeze. Ideally, it should be caught and frozen on the same day, and certainly within 24 hours. Likely sources of supply are sea or river fish caught by family anglers, or for those who live near the sea, a local inshore fisherman who sells direct.

The fish should be kept iced or refrigerated during any short journey home and whilst being prepared for the freezer. Generally speaking, the best results come from freezing fish raw, and fish in season and, therefore, in prime condition.

The freshness of shellfish is even more important; they must be frozen the same day they are taken from the water.

Oysters and mussels offered for sale in Great Britain must have been cleansed and purified in salt water according to Public Health Authority Regulations. Some varieties of shellfish are better cooked before freezing.

ICE GLAZING

The cold air in the freezer has an intensely drying effect from which the fish must be protected. A natural and simple method of doing this is by encasing it in a layer of ice. This is a useful method when no suitable packaging materials are available. The fish needs to be handled very carefully throughout, however, since ice is brittle and liable to crack, and, unless overwrapped, ice glazing alone cannot be recommended for other than very short-term storage.

To glaze, place the prepared but unwrapped fish separately in the freezer (previously set at 'Fast-Freeze' or 'Coldest') and leave until frozen solid. Remove and dip in cold fresh water; a thin film of ice will form over the entire fish. Immediately return to the freezer. Repeat about three times at 30 minute intervals.

STORING FROZEN FISH

Fish is stored commercially at –30°C (–20°F, or 52 degrees of frost on the Fahrenheit scale). The average storage temperature operating in a home freezer or three star domestic refrigerator is only –18°C/0°F, so do not keep fish for long periods. It will not go bad, but it will lose its 'fresh caught' flavour and texture, and oily fish, in particular, may develop rancid flavours. Remember to date-label packages clearly so that you can see at a glance how long they have been in store.

THAWING FROZEN FISH

Unless you are dealing with large whole fish or large portions for deep fat frying, there is no need to thaw fish prior to cooking. Simply separate the small white fish or fillets, and cook from the frozen or partially frozen state. When thawing is necessary, allow 5–6 hours per 450g/1 lb in a cold place or domestic refrigerator and between 3–4 hours at room temperature. Once thawed, use promptly.

Type	Preparation	Methods	High quality storage life	Thawing/ Reheating Instructions
White fish (cod, plaice, sole, whiting)	Clean, leave whole, fillet or cut into steaks.	a) Wrap large fish in freezer paper or polythene. b) Pack small whole fish individually or side by side in single layers to form flat package, with separators of double thickness clingfilm. Wrap in freezer paper or in box or bag.	a) 3 months b) 3 months	a) Thaw large fish, unopened, in refrigerator. b) Cook small fish and pieces from frozen.
Fatty fish (haddock, halibut, mackerel, salmon, trout, turbot)	Clean, leave whole, fillet or cut into steaks.	a) Wrap large fish in freezer paper or polythene. b) Pack small whole fish individually or side by side in single layers to form flat package, with separators of double thickness clingfilm. Wrap in freezer paper or in box or bag. **Note** Freeze large fish singly. Do not use brine packs.	2 months	a) Thaw large fish, unopened, in refrigerator. b) Cook small fish and pieces from frozen.
Smoked fish (bloaters, eel, haddock, kippers, mackerel, salmon, sprats, trout)	Clean, leave whole, fillet or cut into steaks.	Pack raw or cooked fish in layers with clingfilm separators. Do not re-freeze commercially frozen fish. Wrap in freezer paper or in polythene bag or box.	2 months	To eat cold, thaw in refrigerator. Cook haddock and kippers from frozen.
Crab	Must be absolutely fresh, and freshly boiled. Cool. Leave in shell or dress.	a) Closely wrap whole crab in heavy gauge polythene or foil. b) Remove crabmeat from shell, pack meat in containers, or in washed shell. Cover with greaseproof paper, then overwrap in polythene or foil.	1 month	Thaw for 6–8 hours in refrigerator.
Lobster	Must be absolutely fresh, and freshly boiled. Cool. Split shell, remove tail and claw meat, cut into neat pieces, or leave whole.	a) Closely wrap whole lobster in heavy gauge polythene or foil. b) Pack pieces in polythene bag or container.	1 month	Thaw for 6–8 hours in refrigerator.

Chart *continues over.*

Type	Preparation	Methods	High quality storage life	Thawing/ Reheating Instructions
Norway lobsters (scampi, Dublin Bay prawns)	Must be very fresh. Handle raw: twist off heads and carapace with legs and claws attached. Wash tails.	Pack tightly in suitable containers or heavy gauge polythene bags.	1 month	Lower frozen tails into boiling salted water, bring back to boiling point, then simmer for 4–6 minutes. Cool, serve.
Shrimps, prawns	Must be very fresh. Cook or leave raw. Remove heads, leave tails in shells. Wash in salted water, then drain.	a) Cook by dropping into slightly salted boiling water, then simmering for 2–4 minutes. b) Wash cooked prawns in fresh cold water, then boil in lightly salted water for 2–4 minutes. Cool in liquid. Pack prawns and shrimps in cartons or bags.	1 month	Thaw in refrigerator and serve cold, or add to cooked dishes.
Scallops, Queens	Freeze same day taken from water. Scrub shells thoroughly. Open shells by placing in hot oven briefly. Discard black fringe around scallop. Wash fish in salted water. Cut fish, with orange roe, away from shell, then rinse and drain.	Pack into containers, cover, seal.	1 month	a) Thaw, overnight, in refrigerator, then cook as fresh scallops. b) Put frozen into hot water or sauce, and cook.
Oysters	Freeze same day taken from water. Wash shell, open over muslin strainer to catch juice. Wash oysters in salted water. Drain. Usually frozen raw.	Pack in containers with juices.	1 month	Thaw, unopened, in refrigerator for 6–8 hours. Serve raw, or add frozen to hot soup or sauce. Cook 4–6 minutes.
Mussels	Scrub shells, then remove fibrous material from shell.	Put mussels in large pan and cover with damp cloth; cook over medium heat for 3 minutes to open. Cool in pan, then remove from shells, and pack in boxes with juice from pan.	1 month	Thaw in container in refrigerator. Use as fresh fish.

All fish and shellfish must be very fresh when being prepared for freezing

VEGETABLES

Vegetables for freezing must be as fresh as possible.

PREPARATION

1   Check that the freezer can cope with the amount of vegetables you want to freeze. 1.35kg/3 lb of fresh food to each 28.3 litres/cubic foot of freezer space every 6 hours is the usual allowance.
2   Adjust fast-freeze switch where available at least 6 hours before beginning freezing.
3   Wash vegetables in cold water and grade them for size. Prepare and freeze them quickly.

BLANCHING

It is absolutely vital to blanch vegetables (ie subject them to heat treatment) before freezing, to retard enzyme action. This action will cause loss of colour, flavour and nutritive value. Timing must be checked carefully as under-blanching results in loss of nutritive value and colour change. Over-blanching results in loss of flavours and crisp texture.

1   Use a large pan holding at least 4.8 litres/8 pints water, with a lid.
2   Use a blanching basket, wire salad basket, or muslin bag which will hold 4.5kg/10lb vegetables comfortably.
3   Bring water to the boil, adding lemon juice if required.
4   Plunge in the basket of vegetables, cover and bring quickly to the boil again.
5   Time blanching from the second when the water is boiling again.
6   Remove vegetables immediately blanching time is complete, and plunge them into plenty of ice-cold water.
7   Cool completely. If not cooled, they will continue cooking and become mushy.
8   Drain very thoroughly before open freezing or packing.
9   Boil water again before blanching another batch of vegetables.

OPEN FREEZING

After blanching, peas, beans, sprouts and other small vegetables can be open frozen (see page 28). This enables them to remain separate during freezing and they can be shaken out of a package for cooking.

Vegetable	Preparation	Methods	High quality storage life	Thawing/ Reheating Instructions
Note Cook frozen vegetables in very little water, usually 150ml/¼ pint to 450g/1 lb vegetables.				
Artichokes (globe)	a) Remove outer leaves, wash, trim stalks, remove 'chokes'.	a) Blanch in 4.8 litres/8 pints water with 15ml/1 tablespoon lemon juice for 7 minutes. Cool, drain upside-down. Pack in boxes.	12 months	a) Cook in boiling water for 5 minutes.
	b) Remove all leaves and 'chokes'.	b) Blanch hearts as above for 5 minutes.	12 months	b) Use as fresh for special dishes.

Vegetable	Preparation	Methods	High quality storage life	Thawing/ Reheating Instructions
Artichokes (Jerusalem)	Peel and slice.	Cook to soften in butter, then simmer in chicken stock. Rub through a sieve, then pack in boxes.	3 months	Use as basis for soup with milk or cream and seasoning.
Asparagus	Wash, remove woody parts and scales, grade for size, then cut into 15cm/6 inch lengths.	Blanch small spears for 2 minutes, medium spears for 3 minutes, large spears for 4 minutes. Cool, drain, then pack in boxes.	9 months	Cook in boiling water for 5 minutes.
Aubergines	Choose mature, medium size. Peel, then cut into 2.5cm/1 inch slices.	a) Blanch for 4 minutes, then chill, and drain. Pack in layers separated with paper in boxes.	a) 12 months	a) Cook in boiling water for 5 minutes.
		b) Coat slices in batter or egg/breadcrumb, deep fry, then drain, cool, pack in boxes.	b) 2 months	b) Heat in slow oven or part-thaw and deep fry.
Beans (broad)	Shell.	Blanch for 1½ minutes, then pack in bags or boxes.	12 months	Cook in boiling water for 8 minutes.
Beans (French)	Top and tail, leave small beans whole; cut larger beans into 2.5cm/1 inch pieces.	a) Blanch whole beans for 3 minutes.	a) 12 months	a) Cook whole beans in boiling water for 7 minutes.
		b) Blanch cut beans for 5 minutes.	b) 12 months	b) Cook cut beans for 5 minutes.
Beans (runner)	Cut in pieces. Do not shred.	Blanch for 2 minutes, then cool, pack.	12 months	Cook in boiling water for 7 minutes.
Beetroot	Choose young beetroots. Cook in boiling water until tender. Rub off skins.	Pack in boxes, sliced or whole.	6 months	Thaw for 2 hours in refrigerator. Drain, then add dressing.
Broccoli	Choose heads with 2.5cm/1 inch stalks. Trim stalks, remove leaves, wash, soak in salt water for 30 minutes, then wash in fresh water, and cut into sprigs.	Blanch thin stems for 3 minutes, thick stems for 4 minutes. Pack into boxes or bags, alternating heads.	12 months	Cook in boiling water for 8 minutes.
Brussels sprouts	Grade sizes; remove outer leaves, trim stalks, wash.	Blanch small for 3 minutes, medium for 4 minutes. Cool, pack in bags or boxes. Overwrap.	12 months	Cook in boiling water for 8 minutes.

Chart *continues over.*

Vegetable	Preparation	Methods	High quality storage life	Thawing/ Reheating Instructions
Cabbage, green and red	Wash and shred finely.	Blanch for 1½ minutes, then pack in bags.	6 months	Cook in boiling water for 8 minutes (do not use raw).
Carrots	Wash and scrape, leave whole, dice or slice.	Blanch small whole carrots, diced or sliced for 3 minutes.	12 months	Cook in boiling water for 8 minutes.
Cauliflower	Wash, break into sprigs.	Blanch in 4.8 litres/8 pints water with 15ml/1 tablespoon lemon juice for 3 minutes. Cool, then pack in lined boxes or bags.	6 months	Cook in boiling water for 10 minutes.
Celery	Scrub well, string, cut into 2.5cm/1 inch lengths.	Blanch for 2 minutes, then cool, drain, pack in bags.	6 months	Use as vegetable for soups, stews. Do not use raw.
Chestnuts	Boil unshelled, then peel.	Blanch, then pack in boxes or bags with water used for blanching.	6 months	Cook in boiling water or milk, according to recipe.
Chicory	Wash well, remove outer leaves.	Blanch for 3 minutes, then cool in liquid. Pack in blanching liquid in boxes, leaving headspace.	6 months	Put with liquid in covered dish. Heat in moderate oven for 40 minutes, then drain.
Corn on the cob	Use fresh tender corn. Remove leaves and threads, grade for size.	a) Blanch small cobs for 4 minutes, medium for 6 minutes, large for 8 minutes. Cool, dry. Pack individually in foil or freezer paper. Freeze, pack in bags, leaving headspace. b) Blanch, scrape off kernels. Pack in boxes, leaving headspace.	12 months	a) Thaw, put in cold water, bring to fast boil and simmer for 5 minutes. b) Thaw, unopened, in refrigerator. Cook for 10 minutes in boiling water.
Cucumber	Slice thinly.	Pack in boxes covered with equal quantities white vinegar/water, with 2.5ml/½ teaspoon sugar, 5ml/1 teaspoon black pepper to 600ml/1 pint liquid.	2 months	Thaw, unopened, in refrigerator. Drain, then season with salt.

Vegetable	Preparation	Methods	High quality storage life	Thawing/ Reheating Instructions
Fennel	Scrub well.	Blanch for 3 minutes, then cool in blanching water in boxes.	6 months	Simmer for 30 minutes in blanching water or stock. Slip hard cores from roots when cooked.
Herbs (mint, parsley, chives)	Wash sprigs, leave as sprigs or chop finely.	a) Pack sprigs in bags. b) Pack chopped herbs into ice cube trays. Transfer frozen cubes to bags.	6 months	Thaw at room temperature for sandwich fillings, etc. Add frozen cubes to soups, stews. **Note** Sprigs cannot be used as garnish.
Kale	Remove dry, tough leaves from stems.	Blanch for 1 minute, cool, drain, then chop leaves for convenient packing.	6 months	Cook in boiling water for 8 minutes.
Kohlrabi	Trim, wash, peel. Leave whole or cut into dice.	Blanch whole for 3 minutes, diced for 2 minutes. Cool, pack in boxes.	12 months	Cook in boiling water for 10 minutes.
Leeks	Trim off roots, green stems, and wash well. Cut into even lengths or cut finely.	Blanch coarsely cut pieces for 3 minutes, fine-cut for 1½ minutes. Cool, drain or pack in blanching liquid.	12 months	a) Cook drained leeks in salted water. b) Make into purée, or add to soups, stews. Leeks in blanching liquid make soup.
Marrow and courgettes	a) Cut unpeeled young vegetables into 1.25cm/½ inch slices. b) Peel and seed large marrows.	a) Blanch for 3 minutes, then pack in boxes, leaving headspace. b) Cook until soft, then mash. Pack purée in boxes.	a) 2 months b) 2 months	a) Fry in oil, then season. b) Reheat from frozen in double boiler.
Mushrooms	Wipe, but do not peel. Cut into slices, or leave whole.	a) Blanch for 1½ minutes in 3.6 litres/6 pints water with 15ml/1 tablespoon lemon juice to 450g/1 lb mushrooms. Pack in boxes, cup side down, leaving 3.75cm/1½ inch headspace. b) Cook in butter for 5 minutes (90ml/6 tablespoons to 450g/1 lb mushrooms.) Cool, remove excess butter, and pack in boxes.	a) 3 months b) 2 months	a) Thaw in refrigerator, then cook in butter. b) Add frozen to soups, stews or other dishes.

Chart *continues over.*

Vegetable	Preparation	Methods	High quality storage life	Thawing/ Reheating Instructions
Onions	Skin, chop or slice. Leave tiny onions whole.	a) Pack chopped in small boxes. Overwrap. b) Wrap slices in foil or freezer paper, dividing layers. Overwrap. c) Blanch chopped or sliced for 2 minutes. Cool, drain, pack in boxes. Overwrap. d) Blanch tiny onions for 4 minutes. Pack in boxes. Overwrap.	2 months	Thaw raw in refrigerator. Add to salads while frosty. Add frozen onions to dishes according to recipe.
Parsnips	Trim, peel, cut into strips or dice.	Blanch for 2 minutes. Pack in boxes or bags.	12 months	Cook in boiling water for 15 minutes.
Peas (green)	Shell young peas.	Blanch for 1 minute, shaking basket to distribute heat. Cool, drain, pack in boxes or bags.	12 months	Cook in boiling water for 7 minutes.
Peas (edible pods – mange tout)	Wash well. Remove ends and strings.	Blanch in small quantities for ½ minute.	12 months	Cook in boiling water for 7 minutes.
Peppers (green, red)	a) Wash, remove seeds and membranes, then halve or slice. b) Grill on high heat to char skins, then plunge into cold water, rub off skins. Remove caps and seeds.	a) Blanch halves for 3 minutes, slices for 2 minutes. Pack in boxes or bags. b) Pack tightly in boxes in salt solution (15ml/1 tablespoon salt to 600ml/1 pint water), leaving headspace.	a) 12 months b) 12 months	a) Thaw for 1½ hours at room temperature. b) Thaw in liquid, then drain, and dress with oil and seasoning.
Potatoes	Scrape and wash or peel.	a) Blanch new potatoes for 4 minutes. Cool, then pack in bags. b) Slightly undercook new potatoes. Drain, toss in butter, cool, pack in bags. c) Cook old potatoes, then mash with butter and hot milk; pack in boxes or bags. d) Form mashed potatoes into croquettes or Duchesse potatoes. Cook, cool, pack into boxes.	a) 12 months b) 3 months c) 3 months d) 3 months	a) Cook in boiling water for 15 minutes. b) Plunge bag in boiling water, and leave for 10 minutes. c) Reheat in double boiler. d) Thaw for 2 hours, then heat at 180°C/350°F/Gas 4 for 20 minutes.

Vegetable	Preparation	Methods	High quality storage life	Thawing/ Reheating Instructions
Potatoes *continued*		e) Fry chips for 4 minutes without browning. Cool, drain, pack in bags.	e) 3 months	e) Fry in deep fat while frozen.
Pumpkin	Peel and seed.	Cook until soft, then mash. Pack in boxes.	6 months	a) Reheat in double boiler, add butter and season. b) Thaw for 2 hours at room temperature. Use as pie filling.
Spinach	Use only young spinach. Remove stems, wash leaves.	Blanch for 2 minutes, shaking basket to keep leaves separate. Cool, press out moisture, then pack in boxes or bags.	12 months	Melt butter and cook spinach from frozen for 7 minutes.
Tomatoes	a) Grade, wipe, remove stems.	a) Pack in small quantities in bags.	12 months	a) Thaw for 2 hours at room temperature, (skins slip off when thawed). Grill or use in recipes. Do not use raw.
	b) Skin, core.	b) Simmer in own juice for 5 minutes until soft. Sieve, cool, pack in boxes.	b) 12 months	b) Thaw for 2 hours at room temperature. Use in soups, stews.
	c) Core, cut into quarters.	c) Simmer with lid on for 10 minutes. Put through muslin, cool juice, then pack in boxes, leaving 2.5cm/1 inch headspace.	c) 12 months	c) Thaw in refrigerator. Use frosty, adding seasoning.
Turnips	Choose, small, young turnips. Peel and cut into dice.	a) Blanch for 2½ minutes, then cool. Pack in boxes.	a) 12 months	a) Cook in boiling water for 10 minutes.
		b) Cook until tender, then drain and mash. Pack in boxes, leaving 1.25cm/½ inch headspace.	b) 3 months	b) Reheat in double boiler with butter and seasoning.
Vegetables (mixed)	Wash, scrape or peel, then cut into small even-sized pieces.	Blanch each vegetable group separately (see above for times). Mix, then pack in boxes.	12 months	Cook in boiling water for 7 minutes.

FRUIT

PREPARATION METHODS

Open Freezing

Although fruit can be packed straight into containers or bags for freezing, it often sticks together. If it is first open frozen (see page 28), it will remain separate in the packs, and small quantities can be shaken out when needed.

Dry Unsweetened Pack

Wash fruit in ice-chilled water, drain well and open freeze if fruit is delicate. Pack into bags or rigid containers.

Dry Sugar Pack

Use for fruit which can be eaten immediately on thawing.

1   Wash fruit in ice-chilled water, drain well. Crush or slice if liked.
2   Pack in rigid containers in layers with sugar, using sugar as the top layer and leaving 1.25cm/½ inch headspace before closing.
or
Mix fruit and sugar with a stainless spoon until the sugar has dissolved. Pack in bags or containers, leaving 1.25cm/½ inch headspace.

Syrup Pack

Good for non-juicy fruit, or that which discolours easily. Prepare the syrup with white sugar and water. (Brown sugar discolours the fruit; honey flavours the fruit strongly.) Make up the syrup by dissolving the sugar in boiling water, and then chilling the syrup before using. The type of syrup varies from a mixture of 125g/4 oz sugar to 600ml/1 pint water (which gives a very light syrup) to 625g/25 oz sugar to 600ml/1 pint water (a very heavy syrup). In general, a proportion of 300g/11 oz or 450g/1 lb sugar to 600ml/1 pint water is used, giving a medium syrup most suitable for the majority of fruit. Heavy syrup tends to make fruit flabby. Sometimes the syrup is referred to in a percentage:

Sugar	Water	Type of Syrup
125g/4 oz	600ml/1 pint	20% very light syrup
200g/7 oz	600ml/1 pint	30% light syrup
300g/11 oz	600ml/1 pint	40% medium syrup
450g/16 oz	600ml/1 pint	50% heavy syrup
625g/25 oz	600ml/1 pint	60% very heavy syrup

1   Prepare and chill syrup in recommended proportions of sugar and water. Add lemon juice for fruit which discolours easily. Add vanilla essence to improve the flavour of bland fruit such as pears.
2   Wash and drain fruit. Slice if necessary and drop into water or lemon juice if recommended to prevent discoloration.
3   Pack fruit and syrup into rigid containers, leaving 1.25cm/½ inch headspace.
4   Fill this space with crumpled clingfilm, foil or transparent film to prevent fruit rising and discolouring.

A large variety of fruit can be prepared for the freezer

Fruit Purée

Do not use overripe or bruised fruit. Sieve raw fruit such as raspberries or strawberries which mash easily. Sweeten to taste and pack into rigid containers in quantities which can be used for one meal or recipe. If fruit such as apples or damsons need cooking, use the minimum of liquid, and cook in a covered oven dish for best flavour. Sieve, cool and sweeten before packing.

Fruit Juice

Apple, redcurrant and citrus fruit juice can be frozen, but juices are only worth preparing if there is a glut of fruit.

Apple juice should be made in the proportion of 300ml/½ pint water to 900g/2 lb apples. Do not sweeten as fermentation sets in quickly.

Redcurrant juice should be made from juicy currants just covered in water. This is useful for jam-making later in the year.

Citrus fruit juice should be made from good quality heavy fruit, chilled before the juice is extracted. The juice can be strained or not, as preferred.

Apple or redcurrant juice should be strained through a jelly bag or cloth. All juice should be chilled before being put into the freezer. Freeze in small rigid containers, leaving 1.25cm/½ inch headspace. Juice can also be frozen in loaf tins or ice cube trays, and the frozen cubes can be wrapped in foil or polythene for storage.

Fruit Syrup

Syrups are very easily stored in the freezer, and are useful for drinks, sauces and flavouring for a variety of dishes. Use a standard recipe for preparing fruit syrup. Chill and freeze in small rigid containers, or in loaf tins or ice cube trays, wrapping the cubes for storage. One syrup cube gives an individual serving for sauces or drinks.

THAWING FRUIT

Fruit loses quality and flavour if it stands about after thawing, so only thaw the amount which is needed for one meal. Cooked left-over fruit will, however, keep for some days in a refrigerator.

Fruit which discolours badly is best thawed rapidly with a lid on the container, and unsweetened frozen fruit can be put at once into hot syrup to cook so that discoloration is avoided. Fruit can also be put straight into a pie while it is frozen.

Thaw fruit in unopened containers. Allow 6–8 hours thawing time in the refrigerator, or 2–4 hours at room temperature. These times can be speeded up if the container is placed in a bowl of cold water. Unsweetened packs take longer to thaw than sweetened ones; fruit in dry sugar thaws most quickly.

A lot of juice runs from fruit when thawed, so if the fruit is to be used for pies or cake fillings, add a little thickening such as cornflour, arrowroot or flake tapioca, or drain off any excess juice to use as syrup or sauce.

Fruit	Preparation	Methods	High quality storage life	Thawing/ Serving Instructions
Apples	Peel, core, drop in cold water. Cut into ¹/₁₂'s or ¹/₁₆'s.	a) Dry sugar pack (225g/8 oz sugar and 5ml/½ teaspoon citric acid to 900g/2 lb fruit. b) 40% syrup pack, adding juice of 1 lemon to 900ml/1½ pints liquid. c) Sweetened purée, adding juice of 1 lemon to 900ml/1½ pints liquid.	a) 12 months b) 12 months c) 4 months	a) Use for pies, puddings. b) Use for pies, puddings. c) Use for sauces, fools, ices.
Apricots	Peel, then halve or slice.	a) Dry sugar pack (125g/4 oz sugar to 450g/1 lb fruit) b) 40% syrup pack. c) Sweetened purée (very ripe fruit).	a) 12 months b) 12 months. c) 4 months	a) Thaw for 3½ hours at room temperature. b) Use for sauces, ices. c) Use for sauces, ices.
Avocado pears	a) Rub halves with lemon juice. b) Dip slices in lemon juice. c) Mash pulp with lemon juice (15ml/1 tablespoon to 1 avocado).	a) Wrap in foil, then pack in polythene bags. b) Freeze in boxes. c) Freeze in small containers.	a) 2 months b) 2 months c) 2 months	a) Thaw for 2½ hours at room temperature. b) Thaw for 2½ hours at room temperature. c) Thaw, then season pulp with onion, garlic or herbs.
Bananas	Mash with sugar, lemon juice (225g/8 oz sugar to 45ml/3 tablespoons lemon juice to 3 breakfastcups banana pulp).	Freeze in small containers.	1 month	Thaw for 6 hours, unopened, in refrigerator. Use for sandwiches, cakes.
Black- berries, raspberries	Wash ripe berries, dry well.	a) Open freeze unsweetened, then pack in bags. b) Dry sugar pack (225g/8 oz sugar to 900g/2 lb fruit). c) Sweetened purée (cooked or raw).	a) 12 months b) 12 months c) 4 months	Thaw for 3 hours at room temperature. Use raw or cooked in pies, puddings.
Blue- berries	Washed in chilled water, crush slightly.	a) Open freeze unsweetened, then pack in bags. b) Dry sugar pack (125g/4 oz sugar to 4 cups crushed berries). c) 50% syrup pack.	12 months	Use raw or cooked in pies, puddings.

Chart *continues over.*

Fruit	Preparation	Methods	High quality storage life	Thawing/ Serving Instructions
Cherries	Leave in chilled water for 1 hour, then remove stones.	Pack in glass or plastic containers. a) Dry sugar pack (225g/8 oz sugar to 900g/2 lb stoned cherries. b) 40% syrup pack (sweet cherries). c) 50% or 60% syrup pack (sour cherries).	12 months	Thaw for 3 hours at room temperature. Serve cold, or use for pies.
Coconut	Grate or shred.	Moisten with coconut milk. Add sugar if liked (125g/4 oz sugar to 4 breakfastcups shredded coconut. Pack into bags or boxes.	2 months	Thaw for 2 hours at room temperature. Drain off milk. Use for salads, icings, curries.
Cranberries	Wash and drain firm berries.	a) Dry unsweetened pack. b) Sweetened purée.	a) 12 months b) 4 months	Cook in water with sugar from frozen, or thaw for 3½ hours at room temperature.
Currants (black, red, white)	Strip from stems, wash in chilled water, dry gently.	a) Dry unsweetened pack. b) Dry sugar pack (225g/8 oz sugar to 450g/1 lb currants). c) 40% syrup pack. d) Unsweetened purée (black especially).	a) 12 months b) 12 months c) 12 months d) 4 months.	a) Thaw for 45 minutes at room temperature. Use for jams, pies, puddings. b) Thaw for 45 minutes at room temperature. Use for jams, pies, puddings. c) Use as sauce or for drinks, ices, puddings. d) Use as sauce or for drinks, ices, puddings.
Damsons	Wash in chilled water, cut in halves and stone.	a) 50% syrup pack. b) Sweetened purée.	a) 12 months b) 4 months	Thaw for 2½ hours at room temperature. Use cold or for pies, puddings.
Dates (dried)	Remove stones from dessert dates.	a) Pack in bags or boxes. b) Wrap block dates in foil or polythene bags.	12 months	Thaw for 30 minutes at room temperature. Serve as dessert or use for cakes, puddings.
Figs	Choose fresh, sweet fruit. Remove stems. Wash in chilled water. Do not bruise.	a) Peeled or unpeeled in dry unsweetened pack. b) Peeled in 30% syrup pack.	12 months	Thaw for 1½ hours at room temperature. Eat raw or cooked in syrup.

Fruit	Preparation	Methods	High quality storage life	Thawing/ Serving Instructions
Figs *continued*		c) Dried fruit wrapped in foil or in polythene bags.		Thaw for 1½ hours at room temperature. Eat raw or cooked in syrup.
Goose- berries	Wash in chilled water, top and tail, dry. (For pies, etc, freeze ripe fruit. For jam, can be slightly under-ripe.)	a) Dry unsweetened pack.	a) 12 months	a) Thaw for 2½ hours at room temperature or put in pies, cooked from frozen.
		b) 40% syrup pack.	b) 12 months	b) Thaw for 2½ hours at room temperature or put in pies, cooked from frozen.
		c) Sweetened purée.	c) 4 months	c) Thaw for 2½ hours at room temperature. Use for fools, mousses, ices.
Grape- fruit	Peel, remove pith, cut into segments.	a) Dry sugar pack (225g/8 oz to 2 breakfastcups segments). b) 50% syrup pack.	12 months	Thaw for 2½ hours at room temperature.
Grapes	Wash dry seedless varieties. Skin and de-seed others.	30% syrup pack.	12 months	Thaw for 2½ hours at room temperature.
Greengages, plums	Wash in chilled water, dry. Halve and stone.	40% syrup pack.	12 months	Thaw for 2½ hours at room temperature.
Guavas	Wash, dry, peel, halve.	a) Cook in a little water or pineapple juice, then purée. b) Cook as above. Pack in 30% syrup.	12 months	Thaw for 1½ hours at room temperature.
Kumquats	Wash, dry.	a) Wrap whole in foil.	a) 2 months	a) Thaw for 2 hours at room temperature.
		b) 50% syrup pack.	b) 12 months	b) Thaw for 2 hours at room temperature.
Lemons, limes	Peel and slice.	20% syrup pack.	12 months	Thaw for 1 hour at room temperature.
Logan- berries	Wash, dry well.	a) Open freeze unsweetened, then pack in bags. b) Dry sugar pack (225g/8 oz sugar to 900g/2 lb fruit). c) 50% syrup pack. d) Sweetened (cooked fruit) purée.	12 months	Thaw for 3 hours at room temperature. Use for ices, mousses.

Chart *continues over.*

Fruit	Preparation	Methods	High quality storage life	Thawing/ Serving Instructions
Mangoes	Choose ripe fruit. Peel, slice.	50% syrup with 15ml/ 1 tablespoon lemon juice to 1.2 litres/2 pints syrup.	12 months	Thaw for 1½ hours at room temperature.
Melons	Peel, cut in cubes or balls.	Toss in lemon juice, then pack in 30% syrup.	12 months	Thaw, unopened, in refrigerator. Serve frosty.
Oranges	Peel, cut into sections or slices.	a) Dry sugar pack (225g/8 oz sugar to 3 breakfastcups sections or slices. b) 30% syrup pack. c) Pack slices in slightly sweetened fresh orange juice. (Seville oranges may be frozen whole in skins, and packed in polythene bags for marmalade making.)	12 months	Thaw for 2½ hours at room temperature. **Note** Navel oranges tend to become bitter.
Peaches, nectarines	Peel, halve or slice, brush with lemon juice. (Important to work fast as fruit discolours.)	a) 40% syrup pack. b) Sweetened (raw) purée with 15ml/1 tablespoon lemon juice to 450g/1 lb fruit.	a) 12 months b) 4 months	a) Thaw for 3 hours at room temperature. b) Thaw for 3 hours at room temperature.
Pears	Choose ripe but not overripe fruit. Peel, quarter, core, dip in lemon juice.	Poach in 30% syrup for 1½ minutes. Drain, cool. Pack in cold 30% syrup.	12 months	Thaw for 3 hours at room temperature.
Per-simmons	Wash, dry.	a) Wrap whole fruit in foil. b) Peel, then freeze in 50% syrup with 10ml/1 dessertspoon lemon juice to 1.2 litres/2 pints syrup. c) Sweetened (raw) purée.	a) 2 months b) 12 months c) 3 months	Thaw for 3 hours at room temperature. Use unpeeled raw fruit immediately once it has thawed.
Pineapple	Choose ripe fruit. Peel. a) b) c) Cut into slices or chunks. d) Crush.	a) Dry unsweetened pack with clingfilm separators. b) Dry sugar pack (125g/4 oz sugar to 450g/1 lb fruit). c) 30% syrup pack. d) Mix with 125g/4 oz sugar to 2 cups crushed fruit.	12 months	Thaw for 3 hours at room temperature.

Fruit	Preparation	Methods	High quality storage life	Thawing/ Serving Instructions
Pome-granates	Halve ripe fruit. a) Scoop out juice sacs. b) Extract juice.	a) 50% syrup pack. b) Sweeten to taste. Freeze in ice cube trays, then wrap cubes in foil.	12 months	Thaw for 3 hours at room temperature.
Quinces	Peel, core, slice.	Simmer in boiling 20% syrup for 20 minutes. Cool, pack in cold 20% syrup.	12 months	Thaw for 3 hours at room temperature.
Rhubarb	Wash sticks in cold running water. Trim to lengths.	a) Blanch for 1 minute, then wrap in foil or polythene. b) 40% syrup pack. c) Sweetened (cooked fruit) purée.	a) 12 months b) 12 months c) 4 months	Thaw for 3 hours at room temperature, or cook raw fruit from frozen.
Straw-berries	Choose ripe fruit. Remove hulls. a) Grade for size. b) Slice or lightly crush c) Slice	a) Dry unsweetened pack. b) Dry sugar pack (125g/4 oz sugar to 450g/1 lb fruit). c) 40% syrup pack. d) Sweetened (raw) purée.	a) 12 months b) 12 months c) 12 months d) 4 months	Thaw for 1½ hours at room temperature.

DAIRY FOODS AND FATS

Type	Preparation	Method	High quality storage life	Thawing/ Serving Instructions
Eggs	Use very fresh. Do not freeze in shell. a) *Whole eggs:* Blend lightly with fork, adding 2.5ml/½ teaspoon salt or 7.5ml/½ tablespoon sugar to 5 eggs. b) *Yolks:* Mix lightly with fork, adding 2.5ml/½ teaspoon salt or 7.5ml/½ tablespoon sugar to 6 yolks. c) *Whites:* Mix lightly with fork – no addition necessary. **Note** Measure mixed eggs, noting quantities on labelling. Do not freeze hard-boiled eggs.	Pack in containers according to end use; use wax or plastic containers or waxed cups for individual eggs. Eggs can also be frozen in ice cube trays, then wrapped in foil individually and repacked in polythene.	12 months	Thaw, unopened in refrigerator or at room temperature for 1½ hours. a) and b) Use as fresh eggs quickly as eggs deteriorate after thawing. c) Egg whites will keep up to 24 hours in refrigerator.
Milk	Choose homogenized milk.	Pour into cartons, leaving 2.5cm/1 inch headspace, seal.	1 month	Thaw at room temperature. Use immediately as fresh milk.
Cream	Choose 40% butterfat quality. *Devonshire/Cornish creams:* 15ml/1 tablespoon sugar to 600ml/1 pint cream lengthens keeping time *Thick Jersey creams:* Leave in waxed cartons as supplied for freezing.	Pack in cartons leaving 2.5cm/1 inch headspace.	6 months	Thaw in carton at room temperature. Lightly beat with fork to restore smoothness. Use as fresh cream.
Whipped cream	a) Whip 600ml/1 pint cream with 50g/2 oz icing sugar until stiff. Pipe rosettes on foil-covered board. b) Leave in waxed container for freezing.	a) Open freeze for 2 hours. Working quickly, transfer to polythene bags, then return to freezer. b) Freeze cream in container.	a) 6 months b) 6 months	a) Put rosettes on puddings etc, frozen. Leave to thaw at room temperature. b) Thaw in container at room temperature.
Cheeses: Cheddar	a) Cut into small quantities (ie 225g/ 8 oz or less). b) Slice for freezing.	a) Wrap pieces carefully in foil or polythene, then seal. b) Divide slices with clingfilm separators, wrap and seal carefully.	3 months	Thaw, unopened, in refrigerator for 1½–2 hours at room temperature.

Type	Preparation	Method	High quality storage life	Thawing/ Serving Instructions
Cheeses: Cheddar *continued*	c) Grate.	c) Pack in small containers or polythene bags, then seal carefully.	3 months	Thaw, unopened, in refrigerator for 1½–2 hours at room temperature.
Cream cheese	Does not freeze well, but can be blended with cream for dips.	Pack in suitable containers.	3 months	Thaw at room temperature, and blend with mayonnaise for dips.
Cottage cheese	Choose pasteurized quality. Leave in container.	Freeze quickly in container.	3 months	Thaw at room temperature: cheese may separate in thawing.
Brie, Camembert, Port Salut, Mozzarella, Emmenthal, Parmesan, Derby	Mature to individual taste before freezing.	Wrap in polythene and seal carefully.	2 months	Use as fresh cheese. Thaw, unopened, in refrigerator or at room temperature.
Blue cheeses: Stilton, Danish Blue, Roquefort	Mature to individual taste before freezing.	Wrap in polythene and seal carefully.	2 months	Thaw, unopened, in refrigerator or at room temperature. Inclined to crumble after thawing: best used for salads or toppings, etc.
Parmesan cheese	Use grated.	Pack carefully in polythene bag, then seal carefully.	1 month	Thaw at room temperature.
Butter	a) Leave in original wrapper if firm.	a) Store wrapped inside polythene bags or in foil.	(unsalted) 6 months	a) Thaw required quantity overnight at room temperature. Use within a week.
	b) Form into decorative balls.	b) Open freeze, and store on trays in polythene.	(salted) 3 months	b) Thaw at room temperature.
	c) Cream and blend in flavouring – ie brandy, parsley and other herbs, mustard, horseradish etc. Form into long roll.	c) Wrap roll in foil, then in polythene bag.		c) Cut into slices while frozen.
Margarine	Leave in original wrapping if firm.	Overwrap in foil or polythene.	6 months	Thaw required quantity overnight at room temperature. Use within a week.

Chart *continues over.*

Type	Preparation	Method	High quality storage life	Thawing/ Serving Instructions
Suet (fresh)	Convert to rich cooking fat as follows: Chop or mince suet, put in refrigerator in covered bowl for 24 hours. Put suet in heavy pan over low heat, stirring frequently. When fat is clear and smooth and all fibre, etc, crisp, strain through muslin, and measure. Add half the quantity of vegetable oil, chill quickly, stirring as it hardens.	Pack fat into 600ml/1 pint containers, and seal.	3 months	Use thawed for savoury cooking, pastry etc. As the fat is very rich, slightly less should be used for baking than ordinary cooking fat.

PASTRY

Type	Preparation	Method	High quality storage life	Thawing/ Serving Instructions
Unbaked pastry (flaky, puff or shortcrust)	After making, roll out, then form into square shape.	Wrap in greaseproof paper, and overwrap in foil or polythene.	4 months	Thaw slowly. Use as fresh pastry. Do not return to freezer after cooking.
Baked pastry (flaky, puff or shortcrust)	a) After making, roll out and line foil cases, then bake. b) Form into vol au vents, and bake.	Pack, still in foil cases or in boxes, layered with paper.	6 months	Thaw in wrappings at room temperature before filling. **Note** A hot filling may be used and the cases reheated in a low oven.
Unbaked pies	Prepare to recipe with or without bottom. Do not cut air vent in top. Brush surface of bottom crust of fruit pies with egg white before filling.	Freeze unwrapped, then wrap and seal for freezer.	2 months	Cut vent in top crust. Bake from frozen, allowing 10 minutes extra cooking time.

USING A MICROWAVE COOKER
DEFROSTING

The microwave cooker provides a most useful alternative to thawing frozen food in the refrigerator or at room temperature. Many commercially frozen foods are specially packed for microwaving and instructions are printed on the packets. If the food is packed in foil, however, it should be transferred to a special microwave dish or an ovenware dish before defrosting or reheating (see page 25).

If a cooker is fitted with a DEFROST output, it is a simple matter to time defrosting correctly, but it is always a good idea to check food regularly at short intervals to avoid overheating or the collapse of cream or icing. Before defrosting, loosen any coverings and break up solid blocks to speed up the thawing process.

If a cooker is not fitted with a DEFROST output, follow the cooker manufacturer's instructions.

As defrosting continues, semi-liquid foods such as casseroles or sauces should be stirred occasionally so that the food defrosts evenly. When poultry is being defrosted, the wings and legs should be gradually eased away from the body so that the mass of flesh is less solid. Liquid should be drained off from time to time as it runs out of the food. Once thawing is complete, leave to stand for the manufacturer's recommended time so that the dish equalizes in temperature.

Dishes such as cakes or puddings to be served cold, should be defrosted until just slightly icy, then left at room temperature until completely defrosted so that they do not become lukewarm.

REHEATING FROZEN FOOD

Frozen dishes should first be defrosted, then reheated on HIGH power. Instructions on packages of commercially frozen food should be followed carefully. Food packed in boil-in-bag packaging may be reheated in that packaging if the bag is put on to a suitable plate and a small slit cut in the bag. If in doubt, consult the cooker manufacturer's instructions.

RECIPES

SOUPS

Most soups freeze well, though it is often necessary to adjust recipes to suit freezer conditions. Soup which is thickened with ordinary flour tends to curdle on reheating; cornflour is, therefore, best used as a thickening agent since it gives a creamy result. Porridge oats can be used for thicker meat soups. Starchy foods such as rice, pasta, barley and potatoes become slushy when frozen in liquid, and should be added during the final reheating after freezing. It is also better to omit milk or cream from frozen soups; they can be added when reheating.

Large quantities of soup can be frozen in loaf tins or freezer boxes lined with foil; the solid block can then be wrapped in foil and stored like a brick.

Soups will thicken during freezing, and allowance should be made for this in the recipe so that additional liquid can be added on reheating without spoiling the soup. Seasonings may cause off-flavours, and it is best to season after thawing.

Minestrone

225g/8 oz lean beef
4 tomatoes
2 stalks celery (with leaves)
1 carrot
1 onion
1 small turnip
50g/2 oz shelled peas
50g/2 oz haricot beans
   (see **Note**)
1.2 litres/2 pints water
salt and pepper

FOR SERVING
50g/2 oz pasta
grated Parmesan cheese

Mince the meat, using a coarse screen. Put the finely chopped tomatoes, celery tops, carrot, onion and turnip into a pan with the meat, peas, celery stalks cut into 1.25cm/½ inch pieces and the haricot beans. Add the water, bring to the boil and simmer for 1 hour. Season lightly with salt and pepper, cool and pack in containers, leaving headspace, then freeze.

Note The haricot beans need to be boiled briskly in fresh water for at least 10 minutes after soaking overnight.

TO SERVE
Reheat and add the pasta which has been cooked in a separate pan for 5 minutes. Simmer for 10 minutes and serve with plenty of grated Parmesan cheese.
HIGH QUALITY STORAGE LIFE   2 months

Beetroot soup

Beetroot Soup

350g/12 oz cooked beetroot
1 medium onion
450ml/¾ pint chicken stock
3 celery leaves
2.5ml/½ teaspoon salt
pepper
30ml/3 dessertspoons
    lemon juice
5ml/1 teaspoon clear honey
1 egg

Dice the beetroot and put into the liquidizer with the chopped onion, stock, celery, salt and pepper. Blend until the beetroot is finely chopped. Put into a pan and simmer for 10 minutes. Add the lemon juice, beaten egg and honey, and leave until cold. Pack into containers, leaving headspace, and freeze.

TO SERVE
Reheat gently, or thaw and serve cold.
HIGH QUALITY STORAGE LIFE   2 months

Carrot Soup

450g/1 lb carrots
600ml/1 pint water
25g/1 oz butter
3 large tomatoes
salt and pepper

FOR SERVING
600ml/1 pint milk
chopped parsley

Cook the carrots for 30 minutes in the water. Drain, reserving the liquid, and then grate the carrots. Melt the butter and lightly cook the skinned and pipped tomatoes. Add the grated carrot and cook until all the butter is absorbed. Add the carrot cooking liquid and simmer for 30 minutes. Season lightly with salt and pepper, and cool. Pack in a rigid container, leaving headspace, and freeze.

TO SERVE
Reheat gently and when completely thawed, add 600ml/1 pint milk. Simmer until hot and adjust seasoning to taste, then garnish with chopped parsley.
HIGH QUALITY STORAGE LIFE   2 months

Celery Soup

450g/1 lb celery
1 small onion
1.2 litres/2 pints chicken
    stock
15ml/1 tablespoon chopped
    parsley

FOR SERVING
2 egg yolks
150ml/¼ pint single cream
salt and pepper
chopped parsley

Cut the celery into short lengths and chop the onion. Bring the stock to the boil, and add the celery, onion and parsley. Cover and simmer for 30 minutes. Sieve or liquidize until smooth, and cool. Pack into a rigid container, leaving headspace, and freeze

TO SERVE
Reheat gently until hot. Whip the egg yolks with the cream. Add a little of the soup to the cream mixture and stir well. Gradually add the cream mixture to the soup and heat gently, but do not boil. Season to taste and serve hot with a garnish of chopped parsley.
HIGH QUALITY STORGE LIFE   2 months

Oxtail Soup

1 oxtail
seasoned flour
butter
1.5 litres/2½ pints water
2 carrots
2 onions
1 turnip
1 stick celery
25g/1 oz pearl barley
salt

FOR SERVING
2.5ml/½ teaspoon
    Worcestershire sauce
2.5ml/½ teaspoon lemon
    juice

Wipe the oxtail and cut into pieces. Toss in a little seasoned flour and fry in a little butter for 10 minutes. Put in a pan with the water and simmer for 2 hours. Remove meat from bones and return to the stock with the vegetables cut in neat pieces, and pearl barley; season to taste. Simmer for 45 minutes and put through a sieve, or liquidize. Cool and remove fat from the top. Pack in containers, leaving headspace, and freeze.

TO SERVE
Reheat gently in a saucepan, adding Worcestershire sauce and lemon juice.
HIGH QUALITY STORAGE LIFE   2 months

Onion Soup

675g/1½ lb onions
50g/2 oz butter
1.8 litres/3 pints beef stock
salt and pepper
30ml/2 tablespoons
    cornflour

Slice the onions finely and cook gently in the butter until soft and golden. Add the stock and seasoning, bring to the boil, then simmer for 20 minutes. Thicken with cornflour mixed with a little water. Simmer for a further 5 minutes. Cook and skim off any surplus fat. Pack into rigid containers, leaving headspace, and freeze.

TO SERVE
Reheat gently, stirring well.
HIGH QUALITY STORAGE LIFE   2 months

Spring Chicken Soup

1.35kg/3 lb chicken
2 sticks celery
1 leek
1 carrot
125g/4 oz peas (fresh or
    frozen)
salt and pepper

Remove the giblets from the chicken. Put the chicken into a saucepan, cover with water and bring to the boil. Reduce the heat and simmer for 1 hour. Remove from the cooking liquid and cut the flesh into neat pieces (some of the chicken breast could be used for another meal). Cut the celery and leek into neat pieces and slice the carrot into thin rings. Add to the cooking liquid with the chicken flesh and simmer for 15 minutes. Add the peas and simmer again for 5 minutes. Season lightly and then cool. Pour into a rigid container and freeze, leaving headspace.

TO SERVE
Reheat gently, adjust seasoning and serve hot.
For a richer soup, mix 2 egg yolks with a little milk and pour a little of the hot soup into this mixture. Stir the egg yolk mixture into the soup and heat gently but do not boil.
HIGH QUALITY STORAGE LIFE   2 months

Cock-a-Leekie

1 boiling chicken
450g/1 lb shin of beef
6 leeks
50g/2 oz long-grain rice
10ml/2 teaspoons salt
5ml/1 teaspoon black
   pepper
125g/4 oz stoned prunes

FOR SERVING
chopped parsley

Wipe the chicken inside and out and put into a large saucepan. Cut meat into small pieces. Slice leeks thinly, using some of the green parts. Put meat, leeks and rice into the pan. Add salt and pepper and cover with cold water. Bring to simmering point and cook gently for 4 hours. Add the prunes and simmer for 45 minutes.. Take out the chicken and cut flesh into neat small pieces, return to saucepan and reheat. Cool. Pack into containers, leaving headspace, and freeze.

TO SERVE
Reheat gently, adjusting seasoning. Garnish with chopped parsley.
HIGH QUALITY STORAGE LIFE   2 months

Green Pea Soup

900g/2 lb green peas (frozen
   or fresh)
25g/1 oz butter
1 small onion
1 small lettuce
a pinch of mixed herbs
1.8 litres/3 pints chicken
   stock
salt and pepper

FOR SERVING
45ml/3 tablespoons single
   cream

Put the peas, butter, finely chopped onion, shredded lettuce and herbs in a pan with a tight-fitting lid and simmer for 10 minutes. Add the stock, salt and pepper and simmer for 1 hour. Put through a sieve or liquidize until smooth, and cool. Pack in a rigid container, leaving headspace, then freeze.

TO SERVE
Reheat gently and adjust seasoning to taste. Stir in the single cream just before serving.
   If liked, fried or toasted bread cubes, or small pieces of crisp bacon can be used to garnish the soup.
HIGH QUALITY STORAGE LIFE   2 months

Italian Tomato Soup

2 medium onions
1 garlic clove
30ml/2 tablespoons olive oil
900g/2 lb ripe tomatoes
salt and pepper
5ml/1 teaspoon sugar
a pinch of mint
a pinch of basil
a pinch of marjoram
1.2 litres/2 pints beef stock

FOR SERVING
50g/2 oz cooked long grain
   rice
25g/ 1 oz grated Parmesan
   cheese

Chop the onions finely and crush the garlic. Cook them in the oil until soft and golden. Add the peeled tomatoes cut into pieces, with salt, pepper, sugar and herbs. Cover with the stock and simmer for 30 minutes. Put through a sieve, cool and pack in a rigid container, leaving headspace, then freeze.

TO SERVE
Reheat gently and add the cooked rice. Just before serving, sprinkle with cheese.
HIGH QUALITY STORAGE LIFE   2 months

Cock-a-Leekie

Leek Soup

4 large leeks
25g/1 oz butter
1.8 litres/3 pints water *or*
   chicken stock
450g/1 lb potatoes
salt and pepper
a pinch of nutmeg

FOR SERVING
150ml/¼ pint single cream
chopped parsley or chives
   (optional)

Cut the leeks in thin rings and cook in the butter over low heat until they begin to soften. Add the water or stock, sliced potatoes and seasonings. Cover and simmer until the vegetables are soft. Blend until smooth. Cool, pack in a rigid container, leaving headspace, and freeze.

TO SERVE
Reheat gently and just before serving stir in the cream. Garnish with chopped parsley or chives if liked, and serve with cubes of toasted or fried bread, or with French bread.
HIGH QUALITY STORAGE LIFE   2 months

Scotch Broth

450g/1 lb lean neck of
   mutton
2.4 litres/4 pints water
1 leek
2 sticks celery
1 onion
1 carrot
1 turnip
a sprig or parsley
salt and pepper

FOR SERVING
30ml/2 tablespoons pearl
   barley

Cut the meat into small squares and simmer in water for 1 hour. Add the diced vegetables, parsley and seasoning, and continue cooking gently for 1½ hours. Cool and remove the fat on the top. Take out the parsley. Pack into containers, leaving headspace, and freeze.

TO SERVE
Reheat gently in saucepan and add the barley, simmering until it is tender.
HIGH QUALITY STORAGE LIFE   2 months

Basic Chicken Stock

1 chicken carcass
1 carrot
1 onion
1 stick celery
a sprig of parsley
1.2 litres/2 pints water
a pinch of salt

Break up the carcass and slice the vegetables. Put in a pan with water and salt. Simmer for 2 hours, strain and cool, removing the fat from the surface. Pack into foil lined containers, leaving headspace, and freeze.

TO SERVE
Thaw in a saucepan over low heat and add to dishes as required.
HIGH QUALITY STORAGE LIFE   2 months

FISH AND SHELLFISH

Fish is a perishable food and must be dealt with promptly. Neither cooked nor raw fish must be left standing at room temperature, nor kept for more than a few hours in a domestic refrigerator before freezing.

COOKING FROZEN FISH – GENERAL POINTS

Use any of the methods normally used for wet fish but allow a rather longer time at a lower temperature. The actual time will vary according to the thickness of the fish and to the degree of thaw when cooking commences. When the flakes separate easily in the centre of the fish you know it is cooked right through. Take care not to overcook and thus lose the succulence and flavour which correct freezing and storing will have preserved.

Note To make it easy to separate the fillets, consumer packs of commercially frozen fish are interleaved with plastic film dividers. For the benefit of freezer owners, a similar system applies to bulk packs (known as 'shatter packs' in the trade) and these or individually loose frozen fillets packed in bags are the ones to look for when shopping at the frozen food centres. From either pack you can take the exact number of fillets needed for cooking at any one time and leave the rest in the freezer.

Fish Florentine

675g/1½ lb white fish fillet, skinned (see **Note**)
salt and pepper
450g/1 lb frozen leaf spinach *or* 675g/1½ lb fresh spinach (see **Note**)
300ml/½ pint white sauce (25g/1 oz butter, 25g/1 oz flour, 300ml/½ pint milk)
30ml/2 tablespoons grated Parmesan *or* dry Cheddar cheese
a shake of Cayenne pepper
salt and pepper
50g/2 oz grated Cheddar cheese

Divide the fish into 4 portions, season lightly and bake or steam until just cooked. Drain and allow to cool. Cook the frozen spinach according to the directions on the packet. If fresh spinach is used, wash thoroughly, then cook without additional water in covered pan. Drain very thoroughly, pressing out as much water as possible. Season lightly, and leave to cool.

Add the 30ml/2 tablespoons cheese and seasoning to the white sauce, and cook gently for 2–3 minutes. Arrange the spinach to cover the bottom of a lightly buttered foil baking dish. Place the fish portions on top, and coat evenly with the cheese sauce. Sprinkle the surface with grated Cheddar cheese. When quite cold, cover the dish with foil, and freeze.

Note This dish freezes very successfully provided it is made with freshly cooked white fish. The spinach too should be freshly cooked and well drained and dried.

TO SERVE
Heat with the foil cover in a moderate oven, 180°C/350°F/Gas 4, for 20 minutes.
HIGH QUALITY STORAGE LIFE   1 month

Kedgeree

125g/4 oz long grain rice
  (see **Note**)
225g/8 oz cooked smoked
  haddock fillet
50g/2 oz butter
10ml/2 teaspoons lemon
  juice
salt and pepper
15ml/1 tablespoon chopped
  fresh parsley

FOR SERVING
chopped hard-boiled egg
chopped parsley

Cook the rice in plenty of fast boiling salted water until just tender. Drain and spread out to dry and cool. Free the haddock of all skin and bone, and flake the fish coarsely. When both are quite cold, mix together the rice and haddock thoroughly, and add the other ingredients. Fill into a suitable container, seal, and freeze.

Note Use a firm rice which retains its texture, and take care not to overcook it. Cook the rice in plain salted water, not in the liquid in which the fish was cooked.

TO SERVE
Heat gently, breaking up the frozen block with a fork. Cover, and cook over low heat. Pile on to a hot serving dish and garnish with chopped hard-boiled egg and parsley.
HIGH QUALITY STORAGE LIFE   1 month

Fish Puffs

125g/4 oz plain flour
2.5ml/½ teaspoon salt
15ml/1 tablespoon cooking
  oil
150ml/¼ pint lukewarm
  water
225g/8 oz flaked cooked
  fish
15ml/1 tablespoon lemon
  juice
30ml/2 tablespoons
  chopped capers
2 stiffly beaten egg whites
fat *or* oil for deep frying

Sift together the flour and salt and then mix to a thick batter with the oil and water. Add the fish, lemon juice and capers. Fold in the egg whites. Deep fry dessertspoonfuls of the mixture in hot fat or oil and cook until the puffs are golden-brown and crisp. Cool, pack in polythene bags and freeze.

TO SERVE
Thaw for 30 minutes at room temperature, then fry in hot oil or fat until crisp.
HIGH QUALITY STORAGE LIFE   1 month

Fish Rarebit

350g/12 oz white fish fillet,
  skinned
salt and pepper
125g/4 oz coarsely grated
  Cheddar cheese

Arrange the fish in a lightly oiled shallow ovenproof dish. Season. Sprinkle thickly with grated cheese to cover the fish completely. Grill gently until the fish is lightly cooked and the topping golden. This will take from 5–8 minutes, depending on the thickness of the fish. Leave in a cool place to cool quickly. When quite cold, cover with foil and freeze immediately.

TO SERVE
Uncover, and put into a fairly hot oven, preheated to 200°C/400°F/Gas 6, for 30 minutes.
HIGH QUALITY STORAGE LIFE   1 month

Kedgeree

Fish Pie

225g/8 oz cooked halibut
3 tomatoes
125g/4 oz button
   mushrooms
juice of ½ lemon
15ml/1 tablespoon chopped
   parsley
25g/1 oz butter
25g/1 oz plain flour
300ml/½ pint milk
salt and pepper
a pinch of ground nutmeg
350g/12 oz puff pastry
beaten egg

Cut the fish into pieces and arrange in layers with sliced tomatoes and mushrooms in a freezer-proof pie dish or foil container, sprinkling the layers with lemon juice and parsley. Melt the butter and stir in the flour. Cook for 1 minute and blend in the milk. Stir over gentle heat until the sauce thickens. Season with salt, pepper and nutmeg and pour over the fish. Cool and cover with pastry. Brush with beaten egg. Bake in a hot oven, 220°C/425°F/Gas 7, for 30 minutes. Cool and pack in polythene to freeze.

TO SERVE
Reheat from frozen in a moderate oven, 180°C/350°F/Gas 4, for 50 minutes.
HIGH QUALITY STORAGE LIFE   1 month

Fish Cakes

225g/8 oz cooked white fish
225g/8 oz mashed potatoes
10ml/2 teaspoons chopped
   parsley
25g/1 oz melted butter
salt and pepper
beaten egg
breadcrumbs

Flake the fish and mix with the potatoes, parsley, melted butter, salt and pepper; bind with a little egg. Divide the mixture into 8 portions and form into flat cakes. Coat with egg and breadcrumbs and fry until golden. Cool quickly, open freeze and pack in bags for storage.

TO SERVE
Thaw by reheating in the oven or frying pan.
HIGH QUALITY STORAGE LIFE   1 month

Sea Pie

125g/4 oz shortcrust pastry
225g/8 oz cooked cod or
   haddock
125g/4 oz prawns or
   shrimps
25g/1 oz butter
25g/1 oz plain flour
300ml/½ pint milk
75g/3 oz grated cheese
50g/2 oz mushrooms
salt and pepper

FOR SERVING
hard-boiled egg slices

Line a freezer-proof or foil pie plate with pastry and bake blind for 15 minutes. Flake the fish and prepare prawns or shrimps if fresh. Melt butter, add flour and cook gently for 1 minute. Stir in milk, and bring to the boil, stirring all the time. Add fish, prawns or shrimps, cheese, mushrooms and seasoning. Cool slightly and pour into the pastry case. Bake at 200°C/400°F/Gas 6 for 20 minutes. Cool completely. Pack in polythene or foil to freeze.

TO SERVE
Thaw at room temperature for 3 hours to eat cold, or reheat at 180°C/350°F/Gas 4 for 30 minutes to eat hot. Serve garnished with slices of hard-boiled eggs.
HIGH QUALITY STORAGE LIFE   1 month

Fish Lasagne

175g/6 oz green lasagne
450g/1 lb smoked cod *or* haddock
450ml/¾ pint water
1 bay leaf
salt and pepper
1 small onion
1 celery stick
75g/3 oz butter
75g/3 oz plain flour
600ml/1 pint milk
75g/3 oz grated Cheddar cheese

Cook the lasagne in a large pan of boiling salted water for 10 minutes. Drain thoroughly. Put the fish, water, bay leaf and seasoning into a pan and bring to the boil, then simmer gently for 10 minutes. Strain the liquid and reserve. Flake the fish. Chop the onion and celery and fry in the butter until soft and golden. Add the flour and cook for 1 minute. Gradually add the milk and the reserved fish stock. Cook for 5 minutes over low heat, then season to taste and add the grated cheese.

Line a greased freezer dish with the lasagne. Cover with half the fish and one-third of the sauce. Cover with some of the lasagne, the remaining fish and half the remaining sauce. Finish with a layer of lasagne and the remaining sauce. Cool completely, cover with a lid, and freeze.

TO SERVE
Remove the lid and cover the container with foil. Heat in a fairly hot oven, 190°C/375°F/Gas 5, for 45 minutes. Remove the foil and continue heating for 20 minutes.
HIGH QUALITY STORAGE LIFE   2 months

Smoked Haddock Cobbler

450g/1 lb smoked haddock fillet
450ml/¾ pint milk
25g/1 oz butter
25g/1 oz plain flour
15ml/1 tablespoon lemon juice
30ml/2 tablespoons chopped parsley
salt and pepper

TOPPING
50g/2 oz butter
225g/8 oz self-raising flour
1.25ml/¼ teaspoon salt
5ml/1 teaspoon mustard powder
75g/3 oz grated Cheddar cheese
150ml/¼ pint milk

Poach the fish in the milk for 15 minutes and reserve the milk. Flake the fish. Melt the butter, stir in the flour and then the reserved milk. Return to the heat and stir until the sauce thickens. Add the flaked fish, lemon juice, parsley, salt and pepper. Spoon into a greased ovenware or freezer dish.

To make the topping, rub the butter into the sifted flour and salt until the mixture is like fine breadcrumbs. Stir in the mustard and 50g/2 oz cheese. Add enough milk to mix to a soft light dough. Knead lightly and roll out to a rectangle about 22.5 × 10cm/9 × 4 inches. Divide into 6 rectangles and cut each in half diagonally to make triangles. Arrange, slightly overlapping, on top of the fish mixture. Brush with a little milk and sprinkle with the remaining cheese. Bake at 220°C/425°F/Gas 7 for 25 minutes. Cool and wrap in foil or polythene for freezing.

TO SERVE
Reheat from frozen at 180°C/350°F/Gas 4 for 1 hour.
HIGH QUALITY STORAGE LIFE   1 month

Kipper Mousse

275g/10 oz kipper fillets
300ml/½ pint single cream
25g/1 oz butter
25g/1 oz plain flour
300ml/½ pint milk
salt and pepper
2 eggs
15g/½ oz gelatine
juice of ½ lemon
30ml/2 tablespoons water

Cook fresh or frozen kippers by grilling or boiling. Skin the fish and flake the flesh. Mix the kippers with a little of the cream and pound into a paste, adding the remaining cream (or blend in a liquidizer). Melt the butter and stir in the flour. Cook for 1 minute and then gradually add the milk. Stir over low heat until smooth. Remove from the heat, season and beat in the egg yolks. Dissolve the gelatine in the lemon juice and water, and heat until syrupy. Stir into the white sauce and leave to cool slightly before folding into the creamed kipper mixture. Whisk the egg whites to soft peaks and fold into the kipper mixture. Turn into a freezer-proof dish and leave until cold and set. Cover and freeze.

TO SERVE
Thaw in refrigerator for 4 hours and serve with thinly sliced cucumber and brown bread and butter.
HIGH QUALITY STORAGE LIFE   1 month

Halibut in Tomato Sauce

1 large onion
50g/2 oz olives
50g/2 oz mushrooms
15ml/1 tablespoon cooking oil
425g/15 oz canned tomatoes
2.5ml/½ teaspoon mixed herbs
salt and pepper
4 halibut steaks

Fry the sliced onion, olives and mushrooms in oil for 10 minutes. Add the tomatoes, herbs and seasoning and bring to the boil. Simmer for 10 minutes. Meanwhile, grill or fry the halibut steaks and place in a rigid container. Pour the sauce over the fish, cool, cover and freeze.

TO SERVE
Reheat in a cool oven, 150°C/300°F/Gas 2, for 40 minutes.
HIGH QUALITY STORAGE LIFE   1 month

Prawn Quiche

125g/4 oz shortcrust pastry
1 small onion
25g/1 oz butter
175g/6 oz peeled prawns
salt and black pepper
1 egg
1 egg yolk
150ml/¼ pint single cream
25g/1 oz Gruyère cheese

Roll out the pastry and line a flan ring. Bake the pastry blind in a fairly hot oven, 200°C/400°F/Gas 6, for 15 minutes. Grate the onion and fry it gently in butter until yellow. Add the prawns, salt and pepper, and put the mixture into the pastry case. Lightly beat together the eggs, cream and grated cheese, and pour over the prawns. Bake in a moderate oven, 180°C/350°F/Gas 4, for 40 minutes until just firm. Open freeze, then wrap in foil or polythene, or put into a box, and store.

Note This recipe can be made with a mixture of prawns and cooked white fish.

TO SERVE
Thaw at room temperature for 3 hours, or unwrap and reheat in a moderate oven, 180°C/350°F/Gas 4, for 20 minutes.
HIGH QUALITY STORAGE LIFE   1 month

Scallops with Mushrooms

8 scallops
300ml/½ pint dry white
   wine
1 small onion
parsley, thyme and bay leaf
125g/4 oz butter
juice of 1 lemon
125g/4 oz small
   mushrooms
15ml/1 tablespoon plain
   flour
salt and pepper
50g/2 oz grated cheese

FOR SERVING
buttered breadcrumbs

Clean the scallops and put in a pan with the wine, chopped onion and herbs. Simmer for 5 minutes but no longer as they become tough. Drain the scallops, reserving the liquid. Melt half the butter, add the lemon juice and cook the sliced mushrooms until just soft. Drain the mushrooms. Add the remaining butter to the pan, work in the flour, and pour the liquid from the scallops. Simmer for 2 minutes. Season with salt and pepper and add the grated cheese. Cut the scallops in pieces, mix with the mushrooms and a little sauce and divide between 8 scallop shells or individual dishes. Coat with the remaining sauce. Put the shells on to trays, cool, open freeze, then wrap in foil for storage.

TO SERVE
Heat frozen scallops in a fairly hot oven, 200°C/400°F/Gas 6, for 20 minutes, after sprinkling the surface with a few buttered breadcrumbs which may also be frozen.
HIGH QUALITY STORAGE LIFE   1 month

Potted Shrimps

shrimps
butter
salt and pepper
ground mace and cloves

Cook freshly caught shrimps, cool in cooking liquid, then shell. Pack tightly into waxed cartons. Melt the butter, season with salt, pepper and a little mace and cloves. Cool the butter and pour over the shrimps. Chill until cold. Cover with lids, seal and freeze.

TO SERVE
Thaw in containers at room temperature for 2 hours, or heat in a double boiler until the butter has melted and the shrimps are warm. Serve on toast.
HIGH QUALITY STORAGE LIFE   1 month

Seafood Mousse

300ml/½ pint packet aspic
   powder
225g/8 oz cooked lobster,
   crab *or* scampi
15ml/1 tablespoon dry
   white wine
150ml/¼ pint double cream
salt and Cayenne pepper

FOR SERVING
prawns and sliced
   cucumber

Make up the aspic as directed on the packet, but with only 150ml/¼ pint water. Leave until cold. Pound together the shellfish and wine, and put the mixture through a sieve. Gradually add the aspic, a little at a time. Whip the cream to soft peaks and gradually fold into the crab mixture in a bowl on crushed ice. Add salt and Cayenne pepper to taste. Put into individual soufflé dishes, cover and freeze.

TO SERVE
Thaw in refrigerator for 3 hours and garnish with prawns and sliced cucumber.
HIGH QUALITY STORAGE LIFE   1 month

POULTRY AND GAME

POULTRY

Old birds such as boiling fowls are best frozen after being cooked. The meat should be stripped from the bones and frozen; or it can be made at once into pies or casseroles while the carcass is simmering in the cooking liquid, to make strong stock for freezing. Slices of cooked poultry can be frozen on their own or in sauce (the latter method is preferable to prevent drying out). If the meat is frozen without sauce, the slices should be divided by two sheets of clingfilm and then closely packed together excluding air. Roast and fried poultry which is frozen to eat cold is not particularly successful; on thawing it tends to exude moisture and become flabby.

It is not advisable to stuff a bird before freezing as the storage life of stuffing is only about 1 month. It is better to package stuffing separately.

GAME

Any favourite game recipe can be frozen with little adaptation, but, like poultry, it is not recommended to be eaten cold.

Hot water crust game pies can be frozen for a short time completely baked, but the flavour deteriorates after about 2 weeks, and it is really best to freeze only small pieces of leftover pie if absolutely necessary. If you very much want to freeze such a pie, it is best baked and cooled before freezing, but without the finishing jelly. This jellied stock can be prepared at the same time as the pie and frozen – it can then be heated and poured through the pie lid during the thawing process; this will accelerate deterioration however and the pie will not keep.

Chicken Crumble

175g/6 oz shortcrust pastry
300ml/½ pint white sauce (25g/1 oz butter, 25g/1 oz flour, 300 ml/½ pint milk)
350g/12 oz cooked chicken
15ml/1 tablespoon chopped parsley
12 capers
salt and pepper
25g/1 oz fresh breadcrumbs

Roll out the pastry and line a foil pie dish. Bake blind at 200°C/400°F/Gas 6 for 15 minutes. Heat the white sauce and add the chopped chicken, parsley and capers, and season to taste. Cool completely and put into the pastry case. Sprinkle with breadcrumbs. Cover with foil and freeze.

TO SERVE
Reheat at 180°C/350°F/Gas 4 for 45 minutes.
HIGH QUALITY STORAGE LIFE   2 months

Coq au Vin

2 × 1.35kg/2 × 3 lb
   chicken or chicken joints
225g/8 oz bacon
50g/2 oz butter
50ml/2 fl oz oil
20 small onions
30ml/2 tablespoons brandy
salt and pepper
15ml/1 tablespoon
   concentrated tomato
   purée
600ml/1 pint red wine
a sprig of parsley
a sprig of thyme
1 bay leaf
a pinch of ground nutmeg
1 garlic clove
350g/12 oz button
   mushrooms
25g/1 oz butter
15ml/½ oz cornflour

FOR SERVING
chopped parsley
fried bread

Joint the chicken if using a whole one. Cut the bacon in strips and simmer in a little water for 10 minutes. Drain well. Heat the butter and oil together and fry the bacon lightly until brown. Remove from the pan and brown the onions in the fat. Remove the onions and cook the chicken joints for about 10 minutes until golden on all sides. Add the bacon and onions, cover and cook over low heat for 10 minutes. Pour on the brandy and ignite it, rotating the pan until the flame dies out. Season with salt and pepper, and add the tomato purée, wine, herbs, nutmeg and crushed garlic. Cover and simmer for 1 hour. Remove the chicken pieces and put into a freezer container.

Cook the mushrooms in butter until just tender and add to the chicken pieces. Stir the cornflour into a little water and add to the cooking liquid. Simmer until smooth and creamy. Cool and pour over the chicken and mushrooms. Cover and freeze.

TO SERVE
Transfer the dish to an ovenware container, cover and heat in a fairly hot oven, 200°C/400°F/Gas 6, for 45 minutes. Garnish with parsley and fried bread.
HIGH QUALITY STORAGE LIFE   2 months

Country Chicken Pie

1.8kg/4 lb chicken
3 rashers streaky bacon
15ml/1 tablespoon chopped
   parsley
a pinch of mixed herbs
salt and pepper
cornflour
350g/12 oz shortcrust
   pastry

Remove the giblets from the bird. Put the chicken into a pan with all the giblets except the liver (save that for an omelet or pâté) and just cover with water. Bring to the boil, then reduce the heat and simmer for 1½ hours. Cool and remove the chicken meat from the bones. Arrange the chicken meat in layers in a pie dish which will go in the freezer, along with the chopped bacon, parsley and herbs. Season each layer lightly with salt and pepper. Thicken the chicken stock with a little cornflour and cover the chicken. Cool completely and cover with the pastry. Bake in a hot oven, 230°C/450°F/Gas 8, for 45 minutes. Cool and pack into a polythene bag to freeze.

TO SERVE
Reheat in a moderate oven, 180°C/350°F/Gas 4, for 1 hour, covering the pastry if it becomes too brown. The pie may be frozen with uncooked pastry, and should then be baked straight from the freezer in a hot oven, 230°C/450°F/Gas 8, for 45 minutes, then in a fairly hot oven, 190°C/375°F/Gas 5, for 20 minutes.
HIGH QUALITY STORAGE LIFE   2 months

Chicken Pompadour

225g/8 oz spaghetti
50g/2 oz butter
350g/12 oz cooked chicken
salt and pepper
150ml/¼ pint single cream
1 egg yolk
5ml/1 teaspoon chopped
   parsley

FOR SERVING
tomato *or* mushroom sauce

Cook the spaghetti in plenty of boiling salted water for 10 minutes. Drain thoroughly. Grease a foil pudding basin with half the butter and line it with the spaghetti, twisting it round to fit the basin. Chop the chicken and mix with salt, pepper, cream, egg yolk and parsley. Put into the spaghetti-lined basin and top with the remaining spaghetti. Cover with greased paper and foil, and steam for 1 hour. Cool, and pack in polythene to freeze.

TO SERVE
Put the basin with a covering of foil into a pan of boiling water and steam for 1 hour. Turn out and serve with a hot tomato or mushroom sauce.
HIGH QUALITY STORAGE LIFE   2 months

Farmhouse Chicken

4 chicken portions
seasoned flour
25g/1 oz butter
30ml/2 tablespoons oil
2 onions
2 carrots
1 green pepper
450ml/¾ pint chicken stock
a pinch of tarragon

FOR SERVING
150ml/¼ pint single cream

Coat the chicken portions with the flour. Melt the butter and oil together and fry the chicken quickly until golden on all sides. Transfer to a casserole. Chop the onions, and slice the carrots and green pepper. Cook these in the fat until soft and golden, and add to the chicken. Pour in the stock and add the tarragon. Cover and cook in a moderate oven, 180°C/350°F/Gas 4, for 1¼ hours. Cool, pack in a foil container, cover and freeze.

TO SERVE
Reheat in a warm oven, 160°C/325°F/Gas 3, for 1 hour. Stir in the single cream just before serving.
HIGH QUALITY STORAGE LIFE   2 months

Chicken Croquettes

350g/12 oz cooked chicken
25g/1 oz butter
25g/1 oz plain flour
150ml/¼ pint chicken stock
   or milk
50g/2 oz mushrooms
5ml/1 teaspoon chopped
   parsley
salt and pepper
beaten egg
breadcrumbs

Mince the chicken finely. Melt the butter, work in the flour and add the stock or milk gradually, stirring well. Chop the mushrooms and add them with the parsley to the sauce. Cook for 3 minutes. Add the minced chicken, mix well and season. Turn the mixture on to a plate and cool. Cut into equal-sized pieces and roll into thick finger shapes, or form into flat cakes. Coat with beaten egg, dust with breadcrumbs and fry on both sides until golden. Cool and pack in a rigid container to freeze.

TO SERVE
Cook from frozen on both sides in hot fat until golden and hot right through. Croquettes may also be reheated in a moderate oven, 180°C/350°F/Gas 4, for 25 minutes.
HIGH QUALITY STORAGE LIFE   2 months

Chinese Drumsticks

6–8 chicken drumsticks
15ml/1 tablespoon soy
    sauce
75ml/3 fl oz clear honey
50g/2 oz soft butter

Brush each drumstick with soy sauce. Beat the honey and butter together and completely cover each drumstick with this mixture. Place the drumsticks in a large pan that has been lined with foil and bake in a very hot oven, 230°C/450°F/Gas 8, for 30 minutes. Turn the pieces frequently, being careful not to pierce the skin, and baste with the honey and butter mixture. The honey will turn a rich dark brown and completely seal the skin. Lower the heat to moderate, 180°C/350°F/Gas 4, cover and bake for another 45 minutes. Cool and pack in a polythene bag and freeze.

TO SERVE
Put drumsticks on a baking sheet, and heat in a moderate oven, 180°C/350°F/Gas 4, for 1 hour.
HIGH QUALITY STORAGE LIFE   2 months

Casserole of Chicken Livers

225g/8 oz mushrooms
2 green peppers
45ml/3 tablespoons butter
675g/1½ lb chicken livers
1 bay leaf
salt and pepper
125ml/4 fl oz red wine

FOR SERVING
chopped parsley

Toss whole mushrooms and chopped peppers in 15ml/ 1 tablespoon of the butter. Put the rest in a casserole and slightly brown the livers. Add the mushrooms, peppers, bay leaf, salt and pepper and the red wine. Simmer for 10 minutes. Cool, pack in a rigid container and freeze.

TO SERVE
Reheat in a double saucepan and garnish with chopped parsley.
HIGH QUALITY STORAGE LIFE   2 months

Chicken Liver Pâté

225g/8 oz chicken livers
75g/3 oz fat bacon
1 small onion
25g/1 oz butter
salt and pepper
2 garlic cloves
1 egg

Cut the livers into small pieces and chop the bacon and onion. Cook the bacon and onion in butter until just soft. Add the livers and cook gently for 10 minutes. Mince very finely and season. Add crushed garlic and beaten egg and put the mixture into individual foil containers. Stand the containers in a roasting tin half-full of water, cover and cook in a moderate oven, 180°C/350°F/Gas 4, for 1 hour. Cool completely. Cover containers with foil to freeze.

TO SERVE
Thaw containers in refrigerator for 3 hours and serve with toast.
HIGH QUALITY STORAGE LIFE   1 month

Turkey Roll

350g/12 oz cold turkey
225g/8 oz cooked ham
1 small onion
a pinch of mace
salt and pepper
2.5ml/½ teaspoon mixed
   fresh herbs
1 egg
breadcrumbs

Mince the turkey, ham and onion finely and mix with mace, salt and pepper and herbs. Bind with beaten egg. Put into a greased dish or tin (loaf tin, cocoa tin lined with paper, or a stone marmalade jar), cover and steam for 1 hour. While warm, roll in breadcrumbs, then cool completely. Pack in foil or a polythene bag to freeze.

TO SERVE
Thaw at room temperature for 1 hour. Serve sliced with salads or sandwiches.
HIGH QUALITY STORAGE LIFE   2 months

Duck with Orange

125g/4 oz streaky bacon
1 medium onion
1 carrot
45ml/3 tablespoons plain
   flour
15ml/1 tablespoon
   concentrated tomato
   purée
125g/4 oz mushrooms
450ml/¾ pint stock
60ml/4 tablespoons sherry
1 duck
75g/3 oz butter
juice of 2 oranges
salt and pepper
2 oranges

Cut the bacon in small pieces and put over gentle heat to extract the fat. Remove the bacon pieces, and add the sliced onion and carrot to the fat. Cook over low heat until lightly browned. Stir in the flour and cook till brown, then add the tomato purée and sliced mushrooms. Pour on the stock slowly, and stir in the sherry. Cook very gently until the mushrooms are tender, then strain in this sauce. Joint the duck and fry in butter until golden-brown. Put the duck into a casserole. Pour on the sauce, and the juice of 2 oranges. Season well, cover, and cook in a moderate oven, 180°C/350°F/Gas 4, for 1 hour. Remove the orange skins, and slice thinly. Add to the casserole 15 minutes before the end of cooking. Cool, pack into a rigid container and freeze.

TO SERVE
Reheat in a warm oven, 160°C/325°F/Gas 3, for 1 hour.
HIGH QUALITY STORAGE LIFE   2 months

Duck with Cherries

1.8–2.3kg/4–5 lb duck
50g/2 oz butter
225g/8 oz black cherries
150ml/¼ pint stock
1 wineglass Madeira *or*
   sherry
salt and pepper
10ml/1 dessertspoon cherry
   brandy

Roast the duck with the butter inside. Remove the duck from the tin and pour off fat. Cut the duck into large pieces. Put the stoned cherries, stock, Madeira or sherry, salt and pepper in the roasting tin, bring to the boil and simmer until the cherries are tender. Remove from the heat, stir in the cherry brandy and pour over the duck. Cool. Pack into rigid plastic containers (cherry juice may leak through wax containers), then freeze.

TO SERVE
Thaw at room temperature for 1 hour, and reheat gently in a double boiler.
HIGH QUALITY STORAGE LIFE   2 months

Duck with Cherries

Terrine of Duck

2.3kg/5 lb duck
60ml/4 tablespoons brandy
grated rind and juice of 1
    orange
5ml/1 teaspoon minced
    onion
thyme, parsley, 2 bay leaves
1 duck's liver
225g/8 oz veal
175g/6 oz liver pâté
125g/4 oz lean pork
125g/4 oz fresh pork fat
1 egg
salt and black pepper

Skin the duck, taking care to keep the skin intact, and lay aside. Remove the 2 breast fillets, but do not slice them. Remove the rest of the meat from the carcass, scraping all bones clean. Marinate the breast fillets overnight in a mixture of brandy, orange juice, onion, chopped parsley, thyme and crumbled bay leaves and the grated orange rind. Mince the remaining duck meat together with the duck liver, veal, liver pâté, the pork and pork fat. Stir in the liquid and ingredients of the marinade (take out onion). Add the well beaten egg. Season to taste with salt and pepper. Mix well together and fill the skin of the duck in alternate layers of mixture and breast fillets. Wrap the duck skin around and press into a greased tin, the open side of the skin at the bottom. Cover, place in a pan of hot water and bake in a moderate oven, 180°C/350°F/Gas 4, for 1¼ hours. Remove the cover and weight gently as the pâté cools. Remove surplus fat, unmould and wrap in foil or polythene to freeze.

TO SERVE
Thaw in refrigerator for 8 hours and serve in slices.
HIGH QUALITY STORAGE LIFE   2 months

Hunter's Casserole

3 rashers streaky bacon
4–6 rabbit portions
15ml/1 tablespoon flour
salt and pepper
1 onion
2 medium carrots
125g/4 oz mushrooms
15ml/1 tablespoon
    concentrated tomato
    purée
25g/1 oz butter
900ml/1½ pints water *or*
    stock

Cut the bacon into small pieces and fry them until lightly browned. Dip the rabbit portions in the flour seasoned with salt and pepper, and also fry until lightly browned. Chop the onion and cook until soft and yellow. Put the bacon, rabbit and onion into a casserole. Add the sliced carrots, mushrooms and tomato purée. Stir the flour into the butter in the frying pan and cook until browned. Add to the casserole together with the water or stock. Cover and cook in a moderate oven, 180°C/350°F/Gas 4, for 1½ hours. Cool, pack into a rigid container and freeze.

TO SERVE
Reheat in a moderate oven, 180°C/350°F/Gas 4, for 1 hour.
HIGH QUALITY STORAGE LIFE   2 months

Normandy Rabbit

1 young rabbit
75g/3 oz butter
4 garlic cloves
15ml/1 tablespoon
   concentrated tomato
   purée
300ml/½ pint cider
salt and pepper

FOR SERVING
chopped parsley

Joint the rabbit and soak in cold water for 30 minutes, then drain. Cover with fresh cold water and simmer for 30 minutes. Drain well and remove the meat from the bones in large neat pieces. Fry the rabbit in the butter with the crushed garlic cloves until just golden. Stir in the tomato purée and add the cider and seasoning. Simmer for 10 minutes and cool. Pack into a rigid container, making sure the rabbit pieces are covered with sauce, then freeze.

TO SERVE
Reheat gently on low heat, or in a low oven, and serve garnished with plenty of chopped parsley.
HIGH QUALITY STORAGE LIFE   2 months

MEAT

There is little advantage in freezing pre-cooked joints, steaks or chops as the outer surface sometimes develops an off-flavour, and reheating will dry out the meat. Fried meats tend to toughness, dryness and rancidity when frozen. Any combination dishes of meat and vegetables should include undercooked vegetables to avoid softness on reheating. It is very important that all cooked meats should be cooked quickly for freezing.

Cooked joints of meat may be sliced and frozen to serve cold. Slices should be at least 6mm/¼ inch thick, separated by clingfilm or greaseproof paper, and packed tightly together to avoid drying out of surfaces, then put into rigid containers or bags. Meat slices should be thawed for 3 hours in a refrigerator in the container, then separated and spread on absorbent paper to remove moisture. Ham and pork lose colour when stored in this way.

Sliced cold meat may also be packaged with a good gravy. Both meat and gravy must be cooked quickly before packing. The slices in gravy are easiest to handle if packed in foil dishes, then in bags, as the frozen dish may be put straight into the oven in the foil for reheating. If the foil dish is covered with foil before packaging, this foil lid will help to keep the meat moist in reheating. Heat the frozen dish in a warm to moderate oven for 45 minutes-1 hour.

Meat pies can be frozen completely cooked so that they need only be reheated. Preparation time is, however, saved if the meat filling is cooked and cooled, then topped with pastry to be frozen in its raw state. The time taken to cook the pastry is enough to heat the meat filling, and is little longer than the time needed to reheat the whole pie. If a bottom crust is used, sogginess will be prevented if the bottom pastry is brushed with melted lard or butter just before filling.

*Steak and Kidney Pie
(opposite)*

COOKING FROZEN MEAT

Meat which has been frozen may be roasted, braised, grilled, fried or stewed in the same way as fresh meat. In any roasting process, however, it is best to use a slow oven method (for beef, use 150°C/300°F/Gas 2 and also for lamb; for pork, use 180°C/350°F/Gas 4). Frozen chops and steaks will cook well if put into a thick frying pan just rubbed with fat and cooked very gently for the first 5 minutes on each side, then browned more quickly.

Boiling joints should not be cooked while still frozen or the flavour will be poor and weight will be lost.

Pot-roasting joints may be cooked while frozen. All cut surfaces must be sealed in hot fat to prevent excessive loss of juices.

Boneless joints should not be cooked from the frozen state, as the bone is needed to ensure good conduction of the heat.

Roasting Frozen Joints

A meat thermometer must be used, which indicates when the meat is cooked to the required degree of 'doneness'.

1 Put the joint in a roasting bag and loosely seal with twist-tie, then put in a shallow roasting tin.
2 In a roasting bag, cook the joint at 180°C/350°F/Gas 4. Without a roasting bag, seal the joint at 230°C/450°F/Gas 8 for 20 minutes, then continue cooking at 160°C/325°F/Gas 3 for 60 minutes per 450g/lb.
    Cooking times at 180°C/350°F/Gas 4
       Beef (under 1.8kg/4 lb weight) 30 minutes per 450g/lb + 30 minutes
       Beef (over 1.8kg/4 lb weight) 35 minutes per 450g/lb + 35 minutes
       Lamb (under 1.8kg/4 lb weight) 35 minutes per 450g/lb + 35 minutes
       Pork (over 1.8kg/4 lb weight) 45 minutes per 450g/lb + 45 minutes
       Note Small pork joints should not be cooked by this method.
3 About 15 minutes before the end of the estimated cooking time, plunge the thermometer into the middle of the joint, and check the reading. Read the temperature every 10 minutes until the joint is cooked as liked.

Steak and Kidney Pie

450g/ 1 lb chuck steak
125g/4 oz kidney
25g/1oz dripping
450ml/¾ pint beef stock
salt and pepper
15g/½ oz cornflour
225g/8 oz puff pastry

Cut the steak and kidney into neat pieces and fry until brown in the dripping. Add the stock and seasoning and simmer for 2 hours. Mix the cornflour with a little water. Stir into the hot mixture, and simmer for a few minutes until the gravy is smooth and creamy. Pour into a foil dish, or into a freezer-proof pie dish. Cool, cover with pastry, pack into a polythene bag and freeze.

TO SERVE
Bake from frozen in a fairly hot oven, 200°C/400°F/Gas 6, for 50 minutes until the pastry is crisp and golden.
HIGH QUALITY STORAGE LIFE   2 months

Carbonnade of Beef

675g/1½ lb topside of beef
seasoned flour
50g/2 oz butter
2 onions
300ml/½ pint beer
300ml/½ pint stock
1 garlic clove
1 bay leaf
a sprig of parsley
a sprig of thyme
10ml/2 teaspoons sugar
10ml/2 teaspoons vinegar

Cut the beef in slices and dust with seasoned flour. Melt the butter and colour the beef slightly on both sides. Put into a casserole. In the butter, soften the sliced onions without colouring, then put into the casserole. Add the beer, stock, crushed garlic, herbs, sugar and vinegar. Cook in a warm oven, 160°C/325°F/Gas 3, for 1½ hours. Cool, pack into a rigid container and freeze.

TO SERVE
Reheat in a warm oven, 160°C/325°F/Gas 3, for 1 hour.
HIGH QUALITY STORAGE LIFE   2 months

Beef Mexicano

8 small onions
900g/2 lb stewing beef
seasoned flour
25g/1 oz dripping
400g/14 oz canned
    tomatoes
15ml/1 tablespoon made
    mustard
15ml/1 tablespoon chutney
15ml/1 tablespoon honey
15ml/1 tablespoon cherry *or*
    blackcurrant jam
2 garlic cloves

Peel the onions and leave whole. Trim excess fat off the meat and cut into 5cm/2 inch cubes. Toss the meat in seasoned flour. Heat the dripping in a large pan and brown the meat. Add the tomatoes with their juice, and the mustard, and blend together well. Add all the other ingredients, stir well and adjust seasoning. Transfer to a casserole with a fitting lid and simmer for 2 hours in a warm oven, 160°C/325°F/Gas 3. Cool, pack into a rigid container and freeze.

TO SERVE
Reheat in a warm oven, 160°C/325°F/Gas 3, for 1 hour.
HIGH QUALITY STORAGE LIFE   2 months

Beef and Potato Pie

25g/1 oz dripping
2 medium onions
15ml/1 tablespoon flour
15ml/1 tablespoon curry
    powder
300ml/½ pint stock
450g/1 lb minced beef
salt and pepper
10ml/1 dessertspoon
    tomato chutney
675g/1½ lb potatoes
15g/½ oz butter
25g/1 oz Cheddar cheese

Melt the dripping in a saucepan, and gently fry the thinly sliced onions until soft. Stir in the flour and curry powder, cook for a minute or two, then slowly add the stock. Bring to the boil, lower the heat, and simmer until the sauce has thickened. Stir in the meat, breaking up any lumps. Cover and cook over a low heat for 20 minutes. Add the salt, pepper and chutney, mix with a spoon and cook for another 15 minutes or until the meat is tender.

Meanwhile, peel and boil the potatoes. Drain well, season, stir in the butter and grated cheese, and mash well.

When the meat is ready, transfer to a foil dish, cover with the potato mixture and cook in a hot oven, 220°C/425°F/Gas 7, for about 15 minutes until the potato topping is lightly browned. Cool, cover with a foil lid and freeze.

TO SERVE
Remove the lid and heat in a moderate oven 180°C/350°F/Gas 4, for 45 minutes.
HIGH QUALITY STORAGE LIFE   2 months

Cannelloni

12 cannelloni
5ml/1 teaspoon oil
125g/4 oz streaky bacon
450g/1 lb raw minced beef
1 large onion
50g/2 oz concentrated
   tomato purée
2.5ml/½ teaspoon mixed
   herbs
450ml/¾ pint cheese sauce
   (25g/1 oz butter, 25g/
   1 oz flour, 50g/2 oz grated
   hard cheese, 450ml/
   ¾ pint milk)

Cook the cannelloni as directed on the packet, then drain thoroughly. Heat the oil and fry the finely chopped bacon for 3 minutes. Stir in the beef and onion, and cook for 10 minutes. Drain off the surplus fat. Stir the tomato purée and herbs into the meat mixture. Fill the cannelloni with the meat mixture and arrange in a greased freezer container. Season the cheese sauce well and pour over the cannelloni. Cool, cover with foil or a lid, and freeze.

TO SERVE
Remove lid and bake in a fairly hot oven, 190°C/375°F/Gas 5, for 1 hour.
HIGH QUALITY STORAGE LIFE   2 months

Beef in Cider

675g/1½ lb stewing steak
40g/1½ oz cornflour
salt and pepper
30ml/2 tablespoons oil
2 onions
1 garlic clove
2 carrots
2 oranges
150ml/¼ pint cider
600ml/1 pint beef stock

Trim the meat, cut into cubes and coat in the seasoned cornflour. Heat the oil and fry the meat, sliced onion and chopped garlic. Remove to a casserole. Add the carrots cut into matchsticks. Thinly peel the oranges, remove the white pith, blanch the peel for a few minutes, then cut in thin strips. Add to the meat and vegetables. Squeeze the juice from the oranges and add to the cider. Add the beef stock. Pour over the meat and vegetables. Cover and cook for 1¼ hours in a moderate oven, 180°C/350°F/Gas 4. Cool, pack in a rigid container and freeze.

TO SERVE
Reheat in a warm oven, 160°C/325°F/Gas 3, for 1 hour.
HIGH QUALITY STORAGE LIFE   2 months

Beef with Walnuts

675g/1½ lb topside of beef
15ml/1 tablespoon bacon
   fat
12 small onions
a pinch of sugar
25g/1 oz flour
1 wineglass red wine
1 bay leaf
a sprig of thyme
a sprig of parsley
1 garlic clove
5ml/1 teaspoon salt
stock
50g/2 oz shelled walnuts
25g/1 oz butter
1 celery heart

Cut the meat into large cubes and fry in the bacon fat. Remove to a casserole and fry the onions in the same fat with a pinch of sugar until they start to colour. Work in the flour, cook for 3 minutes, then add the wine. Add to the meat the bay leaf, thyme, parsley and garlic clove crushed with salt. Pour on hot stock to cover, put on a lid and cook in a warm oven, 160°C/325°F/Gas 3, for 1½ hours. After 1 hour, toss the walnuts in hot butter, and add the celery heart cut into small strips. Cook for 3 minutes, then add to the meat in the casserole. Cool, pack in a rigid container and freeze.

TO SERVE
Reheat in a warm oven, 160°C/325°F/Gas 3, for 1 hour.
HIGH QUALITY STORAGE LIFE   2 months

Spaghetti Bolognese

30ml/2 tablespoons oil
50g/2 oz onions
450g/1 lb raw minced beef
400g/14 oz canned
tomatoes
50g/2 oz concentrated
tomato purée
300ml/½ pint beef stock
a pinch of marjoram
1 bay leaf
salt and pepper
450g/1 lb spaghetti

Heat the oil and fry the chopped onions and beef until golden. Add the tomatoes with the juice, purée, stock and herbs, with salt and pepper to taste. Simmer for at least 45 minutes, stirring occasionally. If liked, use a little red wine in place of some of the stock. A chopped chicken liver and a crushed garlic clove give added richness and flavour to the sauce. Remove the bay leaf before freezing the dish.

While the sauce is cooking, cook the spaghetti in a large pan of boiling salted water for about 12 minutes until tender but still firm. Drain very well and put in the middle of a large foil container. Put the sauce round the spaghetti, cover with a lid, and freeze.

Note The pasta in composite dishes should be placed in the middle of the container as it heats more quickly than the sauce and can dry out when reheated. The sauce can be packed separately in a rigid container for freezing, to be paired with freshly cooked pasta.

TO SERVE
Remove the lid and cover the container with foil. Heat in a fairly hot oven, 190°C/375°F/Gas 5, for 45 minutes. If the sauce is frozen separately, reheat it gently in a double saucepan.
HIGH QUALITY STORAGE LIFE   2 months

Cumberland Cutlets

8 best end neck lamb cutlets
oil
1 small onion
1 garlic clove
125g/4 oz mushrooms
1 red pepper
15ml/1 tablespoon
concentrated tomato
purée
150ml/¼ pint stock
15ml/1 tablespoon lemon
juice
10ml/2 teaspoons sugar
salt and pepper

Fry the cutlets in hot oil until brown on both sides. Remove from the pan and place in a casserole. Fry the chopped onion and garlic until soft and the sliced mushrooms until lightly browned. Drain and place in the casserole with the cutlets. Add the sliced red pepper. Mix together with the tomato purée, stock and lemon juice and pour into the casserole. Season with sugar, salt and pepper. Cover and bake in a moderate oven, 180°C/350°F/Gas 4, for 45 minutes. Allow to cool. Put the chops and sauce in foil container, seal, and freeze.

TO SERVE
Reheat in a fairly hot oven, 190°C/375°F/Gas 5, for 45 minutes.
HIGH QUALITY STORAGE LIFE   2 months

Cumberland Cutlets

Burgundy Lamb

125g/4 oz bacon
1 medium onion
1 garlic clove
675g/1½ lb leg *or* shoulder
  of lamb
15ml/1 tablespoon flour
1 medium carrot
15ml/ 1 tablespoon
  concentrated tomato
  purée
125g/4 oz button
  mushrooms
450ml/¾ pint red wine
salt and pepper
5ml/1 teaspoon sugar

Fry the chopped bacon in a large deep frying pan until crisp. Remove from the pan. Fry the sliced onion and crushed garlic in the bacon fat until golden-brown. Cut the lamb into 2.5cm/1 inch cubes, dust with flour, and add to the onion with the sliced carrot. Fry for 10–15 minutes until the meat is brown on all sides. Return the bacon to the pan with the tomato purée, mushrooms, red wine, salt, pepper and sugar, and bring to the boil. Place in a large casserole and cook in a moderate oven, 180°C/350°F/Gas 4, for 1½ hours. Cool, pack into a rigid container and freeze.

TO SERVE
Reheat in a moderate oven, 180°C/350°F/Gas 4, for 1 hour.
HIGH QUALITY STORAGE LIFE   2 months

Savoury Lamb Pie

450g/1 lb fillet of neck of
  lamb
2 large onions
3 lamb's kidneys
5ml/1 teaspoon sage
300ml/½ pint stock
salt and pepper
125g/4 oz button
  mushrooms
flour

PASTRY
125g/4 oz plain flour
50g/2 oz margarine
25g/1 oz grated Cheddar
  cheese
beaten egg

Ask the butcher to cut the fillet from the neck of lamb, and then cut the meat into 2.5cm/1 inch cubes. Fry the lamb in its own fat. Add the chopped onions, chopped kidneys, sage, stock and seasoning. Bring to the boil, cover and simmer for 1 hour. Add the mushrooms and then thicken the liquid with a little flour if a thick sauce is liked. Put into a freezer-proof pie dish or foil container.

Make the pastry with the flour, fat and grated cheese and mix with a little cold water to a stiff dough. Roll out the pastry and cover the pie. Brush with beaten egg and bake in a fairly hot oven, 200°C/400°F/Gas 6, for 30 minutes. Cool, pack in a polythene bag and freeze.

TO SERVE
Reheat in a moderate oven, 180°C/350°F/Gas 4, for 50 minutes.
HIGH QUALITY STORAGE LIFE   2 months

Sweet and Sour Lamb

675g/1½ boned breast of
  lamb
1 medium onion
1 medium carrot
300ml/½ pint stock
15ml/1 tablespoon vinegar
10ml/2 teaspoons cornflour
10ml/2 teaspoons soy sauce
10ml/2 teaspoons brown
  sugar

Cut the meat into thin strips and fry in its own fat until crisp. Drain off the fat. Add the sliced onion and carrot to the lamb with the stock. Add the vinegar, cornflour blended with a little water, soy sauce and sugar. Cover and simmer for 1 hour. Cool and pack in a rigid or foil container to freeze.

TO SERVE
Reheat gently in a double saucepan and serve with rice or noodles.
HIGH QUALITY STORAGE LIFE   2 months

Spring Veal

450g/1 lb stewing veal
50g/2 oz butter
12 button onions
25g/1 oz plain flour
600ml/1 pint beef stock
salt and pepper
a bunch of mixed herbs
225g/8 oz French beans
1 firm lettuce heart
225g/8 oz shelled peas
225g/8 oz new carrots

FOR SERVING
450g/1 lb new potatoes

Cut the meat into cubes. Melt the butter and fry the meat until golden. Lift out the meat and place in a casserole. Add the whole onions to the fat and fry over low heat until golden. Stir in the flour and cook for 1 minute. Add the stock, salt, pepper and herbs, and simmer for 5 minutes. Pour over the veal, stir well and cover. Cook at 160°C/325°F/Gas 3 for 1 hour. Cut the beans in chunks and the lettuce heart into quarters. Add the beans, lettuce heart, peas and carrots to the casserole, cover and continue cooking for 30 minutes. Cool, pack in a rigid container and freeze.

TO SERVE
Return to casserole, cover and heat at 160°C/325°F/Gas 3 for 30 minutes, then add the potatoes and cook for another 30 minutes.
HIGH QUALITY STORAGE LIFE   1 month

Spanish Veal Rolls

4 veal escalopes
125g/4 oz butter
1 medium onion
125g/4 oz mushrooms
50g/2 oz stuffed green
    olives
50g/2 oz fresh white
    breadcrumbs
1 egg
salt and pepper
25g/1 oz plain flour
150ml/¼ pint chicken stock
juice of 1 orange
15ml/1 tablespoon sherry

FOR SERVING
150ml/¼ pint single cream
25g/1 oz stuffed green
    olives

Make sure that the veal is very thin.

Melt half the butter and fry the chopped onion until soft and golden. Add the chopped mushrooms and cook for 2 minutes. Chop the olives and stir into the pan with the breadcrumbs. Remove from the heat and work in the beaten egg, salt and pepper. Spread this mixture on the veal slices, roll up and secure with string. Melt the remaining butter and fry the veal rolls until golden and cooked through. Put into a shallow freezer container. Stir the flour into the pan juices and add the stock slowly, stirring to mix well. Add the orange juice and sherry, and simmer for 1 minute. Pour over the veal, cool completely and cover for freezing.

TO SERVE
Reheat at 160°C/325°F/Gas 3 for 1 hour. Lift the veal rolls on to a serving dish and keep warm. Stir the cream into the sauce and heat gently without boiling. Pour over the veal and garnish with sliced olives.
HIGH QUALITY STORAGE LIFE   1 month

Veal with Olives

450g/1 lb stewing veal
45ml/3 tablespoons olive oil
2 onions
30ml/2 tablespoons flour
½ glass white wine
300ml/½ pint stock
125g/4 oz mushrooms
30ml/2 tablespoons
 concentrated tomato
 purée
1 garlic clove
12 pitted green olives
pepper

Cut the veal in pieces and fry in oil until golden. Slice the onions and fry until golden. Sprinkle in the flour, and cook until brown. Stir in the wine and stock, bring to the boil, and add the sliced mushrooms, tomato purée and crushed garlic. Cover and cook in a warm oven, 160°C/325°F/Gas 3, for 1 hour. Add the olives and a good shake of pepper 5 minutes before cooking finishes. Cool, pack in a rigid container and freeze.

TO SERVE
Reheat in a warm oven, 160°C/325°F/Gas 3 for 1 hour.
HIGH QUALITY STORAGE LIFE   2 months

Tarragon Veal

675g/1½ lb stewing veal
50g/2 oz butter
15g/½ oz plain flour
300ml/½ pint dry white
 wine
15ml/1 tablespoon chopped
 fresh tarragon

FOR SERVING
hard-boiled eggs

Cut the veal into cubes and brown on all sides in the butter. Sprinkle in the flour and cook for 2 minutes. Add the wine and simmer for 2 minutes. Turn into a casserole, cover and cook in a warm oven, 160°C/325°F/Gas 3, for 1 hour. Stir in the tarragon and continue cooking for 10 minutes. Cool completely and pack in a rigid container to freeze.

TO SERVE
Reheat in a warm oven, 160°C/325°F/Gas 3, for 1 hour and serve sprinkled with finely chopped hard-boiled egg.
HIGH QUALITY STORAGE LIFE   2 months

Liver in Wine

350g/12 oz of calf's liver
3 onions
30ml/2 tablespoons olive oil
1 wineglass red wine
1 wineglass water
10ml/2 tablespoons brown
 sugar
1 sprig of parsley
salt and pepper

Cut the liver in cubes, and slice the onions. Heat the oil, and toss the liver and onions quickly until brown. Add the wine, water, sugar, parsley, salt and pepper to taste. Cover and cook in a warm oven, 160°C/325°F/Gas 3, for 45 minutes. Cool, pack into a rigid container and freeze.

TO SERVE
Reheat in a warm oven, 160°C/325°F/Gas 3, for 45 minutes.
HIGH QUALITY STORAGE LIFE   2 months

Cranberry Pork Chops

4 pork chops
salt and pepper
225g/8 oz cranberries
50g/2 oz honey
30ml/2 tablespoons water

Heat a little fat in a heavy pan and brown the chops on both sides. Put them into a foil freezer tray and season with salt and pepper. Crush the cranberries and mix them with the honey and water. Pour over the chops, cover and bake in a moderate oven, 180°C/350°F/Gas 4, for 45 minutes. Cool and cover with a lid for freezing.

TO SERVE
Reheat in a moderate oven, 180°C/350°F/Gas 4, for 45 minutes.
HIGH QUALITY STORAGE LIFE   2 months

Pork and Sausage Plait

125g/4 oz belly pork
225g/8 oz pork
    sausage-meat
salt and pepper
5ml/1 teaspoon basil
beaten egg
225g/8 oz puff pastry

Chop or mince the pork very finely. Mix thoroughly with the sausage-meat, seasoning, herbs and half the beaten egg. Form into a long roll 10cm/4 inches thick. Roll out pastry to an oblong 25cm/10 inches long. Place the meat roll down the centre leaving equal borders cut obliquely in 1.25cm/½ inch wide strips, and brush with beaten egg. Fold alternate strips across the filling to form a plait. Glaze with beaten egg and bake in a fairly hot oven, 200°C/400°F/Gas 6, for 30 minutes. Cool. Cover and freeze.

TO SERVE
Reheat in a low oven, or thaw and serve cold.
HIGH QUALITY STORAGE LIFE   2 months

Pork with Orange Sauce

6 large lean pork chops
seasoned flour
oil
2 medium onions
300ml/½ pint orange juice
30ml/2 tablespoons vinegar
15ml/1 tablespoon brown
    sugar

FOR SERVING
fresh orange slices *or*
    segments

Toss the meat very lightly in a little seasoned flour and cook in a little oil until browned. Remove from the oil and cook the sliced onions until just soft. Return the chops and onions to the pan, pour over the orange juice, vinegar and sugar, and simmer gently for 30 minutes until the chops are cooked through. Cool. Pack in foil trays, cover with sauce, cover with a foil lid and freeze.

TO SERVE
Heat with the lid on in a moderate oven, 180°C/350°F/Gas 4, for 45 minutes. Garnish with fresh orange slices or segments.
HIGH QUALITY STORAGE LIFE   2 months

Bacon in Madeira

50g/2 oz lard
1 carrot
1 turnip
1 onion
900g/2 lb collar bacon in
    one piece
125g/4 oz mushrooms
1 bay leaf
1 sprig thyme
1 sprig parsley
450ml/¾ pint stock
60ml/4 tablespoons
    Madeira

Melt the lard and toss the diced carrot, turnip and onion until lightly golden. Drain and put into a casserole. Put the bacon piece in the hot fat and fry on both sides for 5 minutes. Put on top of the vegetables in the casserole, add the mushrooms, bay leaf, thyme and parsley, and pour over the stock mixed with the Madeira. Cover and cook in a warm oven, 160°C/325°F/Gas 3, for 1 hour. Remove the herbs, cool, pack in rigid container and freeze.

TO SERVE
Reheat in a warm oven, 160°C/325°F/Gas 3, for 1 hour.
HIGH QUALITY STORAGE LIFE   1 month

Farmhouse Pâté

12 rashers streaky bacon
225g/8 oz pig's liver
225g/8 oz stewing veal
1 medium onion
25g/1 oz fresh white
    breadcrumbs
1.25ml/¼ teaspoon sage
15ml/1 tablespoon brandy
    or sherry
salt and pepper
beaten egg

Remove the rind and stretch the bacon rashers by drawing the blade of a knife along them. Cut each rasher in half and use to line the foil pudding basins. Mince the liver, veal and onion, and mix with the remaining ingredients until well blended, then spoon into prepared basins and press down well. Cover each basin tightly with a piece of foil, then place the basins in a roasting tin filled with 2.5cm/1 inch water. Cook in a warm oven, 160°C/325°F/Gas 3, for 1–1½ hours. Loosen the lids, and allow the pâté to cool. Pour off excess liquid, cover the basins with foil, then freeze quickly.

TO SERVE
Thaw in refrigerator for 8 hours or overnight. Serve with Melba Toast.
HIGH QUALITY STORAGE LIFE   1 month

Chunky Pâté

350g/12 oz belly pork
350g/12 oz bacon pieces
40g/1½ oz crustless white
    bread
freshly ground black pepper
2.5ml/½ teaspoon sage
2.5ml/½ teaspoon mustard
    powder
1 egg
45ml/3 tablespoons milk
125g/4 oz liver sausage

Mince the pork, bacon and bread. Mix with the pepper, sage, mustard, egg and milk and beat well. Grease a 450g/1 lb loaf tin and spread in half the meat mixture. Chop the liver sausage in small pieces and cover the meat mixture. Top with the remaining meat mixture. Cover with foil and bake in a moderate oven, 180°C/350°F/Gas 4, for 45 minutes. Strain off excess fat. Continue cooking for 15 minutes. Cool in the tin, then turn out. Wrap in foil or polythene to freeze.

TO SERVE
Thaw in refrigerator for 6 hours, then cut into slices.
HIGH QUALITY STORAGE LIFE   2 months

VEGETABLE AND OTHER LIGHTER DISHES

Mixed Vegetable Casserole

900g/2 lb assorted
  vegetables, eg a mixture
  of carrots, parsnips,
  potatoes, onions, celery,
  peppers and tomatoes
3 rashers bacon
50g/2 oz butter
50g/2 oz flour
15ml/1 tablespoon made
  mustard
300ml/½ pint milk
salt and pepper
75g/3 oz grated cheese

Dice the vegetables and cook in boiling salted water for 10 minutes. Drain and reserve 300ml/½ pint of the vegetable stock. Derind the bacon rashers, cut into strips and dry fry. Melt the butter in a pan, remove from the heat and stir in the flour and mustard. Add the milk and vegetable stock and bring to the boil, stirring continuously. Simmer for 10 minutes until thick. Pour half the sauce on the bottom of a foil freezer dish, add the cooked vegetables and bacon pieces. Season well with salt and pepper and cover with the rest of the sauce. Sprinkle the grated cheese on top. Bake for 20 minutes in a moderate oven, 180°C/350°F/Gas 4. Cool, cover with a lid and freeze.

TO SERVE
Uncover, and heat in a moderate oven, 180°C/350°F/Gas 4, for 35 minutes.
HIGH QUALITY STORAGE LIFE   1 month

Stuffed Courgettes in Tomato Sauce

6 courgettes
1 small onion
225g/8 oz minced cooked
  meat
50g/2 oz fresh breadcrumbs
salt and pepper

SAUCE
400g/14 oz canned
  tomatoes
1 small onion
1 garlic clove
15g/½ oz butter
15g/½ oz plain flour
salt and pepper

Split the courgettes in half lengthways and place in an ovenware dish. Mix the chopped onion with the meat, breadcrumbs and seasoning. Fill the courgettes with this mixture.

To make the sauce, simmer the tomatoes in their juice for 10 minutes, with the finely chopped onion and crushed garlic, and then put through a sieve. Melt the butter and work in the flour. Cook for 1 minute and add the sieved tomato mixture. Season well and simmer for 10 minutes. Pour over the courgettes. Cover with foil and bake for 30 minutes in a moderate oven, 180°C/350°F/Gas 4. Cool and cover with foil to freeze (the dish may be cooked in a foil container and then covered with a card lid if preferred).

TO SERVE
Cover with foil and heat in a moderate oven, 180°C/350°F/Gas 4, for 30 minutes. Remove the foil and continue heating for 15 minutes.
HIGH QUALITY STORAGE LIFE   2 months

Ratatouille

3 small aubergines
salt and pepper
45ml/3 tablespoons olive oil
2 medium onions
2 garlic cloves
4 small courgettes
450g/1 lb ripe tomatoes
2 small green *or* red peppers

FOR SERVING
chopped parsley

Cut the unpeeled aubergines into 1.25cm/½ inch rings. Place in a colander and sprinkle with salt. Heat the oil and cook the chopped onions and crushed garlic until the onions are just soft and golden. Rinse the aubergines and dry the slices on kitchen paper. Add to the onion with the unpeeled courgette slices, skinned tomatoes and diced peppers. Season with salt and pepper, cover and simmer for 45 minutes, stirring occasionally, until the oil has been absorbed. Cool, pack in a rigid container and freeze.

TO SERVE
Thaw at room temperature for 3 hours and garnish with chopped parsley to serve cold. Ratatouille may also be reheated very gently.
HIGH QUALITY STORAGE LIFE   2 months

Bean Casserole

350g/12 oz butter beans
1 glass red wine
350g/12 oz bacon
2 garlic cloves
salt and pepper
350g/12 oz potatoes
275g/10 oz runner beans

FOR SERVING
sliced tomatoes
chopped parsley

Soak the butter beans overnight in water. Drain, then boil briskly in 1.8 litres/3 pints water for at least 10 minutes. Add the wine and bacon, bring to the boil, and simmer for 1 hour. Add the crushed garlic cloves, and season with salt and pepper. Peel the potatoes and slice, add to the pot and simmer for a further 10 minutes, then add the runner beans. Simmer for a further 15 minutes. Leave to cool, put in a rigid container and freeze.

TO SERVE
Reheat thoroughly. Add the sliced tomatoes and chopped parsley 5 minutes before serving.
HIGH QUALITY STORAGE LIFE   2 months

Chicory with Cheese

4 chicory heads
stock *or* water flavoured
    with lemon juice
4 slices of cooked ham
25g/1 oz butter
4 slices Cheddar cheese
25g/1 oz breadcrumbs

Cook the chicory in a little stock, or in some water with lemon juice for 25 minutes. Drain well and wrap each chicory head in a piece of ham. Butter a foil freezer container and put in the chicory and ham. Cover with cheese and sprinkle with the breadcrumbs and flakes of butter. Bake in a fairly hot oven, 190°C/375°F/Gas 5, for 15 minutes. Cool, cover and freeze.

TO SERVE
Uncover and heat in a moderate oven, 180°C/350°F/Gas 4, for 30 minutes.
HIGH QUALITY STORAGE LIFE   2 months

Potato Croquettes

900g/2 lb potatoes
5ml/1 teaspoon salt
a pinch of white pepper
25g/1 oz butter
2 eggs
2 egg yolks
75ml/3 fl oz milk
15ml/1 tablespoon salad oil
40g/1½ oz plain flour
50g/2 oz dry breadcrumbs

Peel the potatoes and cut them in small pieces. Cook them in boiling salted water until tender, and drain well. Shake over low heat until they are dry and then mash them smoothly. Beat in the salt and pepper, butter, 1 egg and the egg yolks. Form into sausage shapes (this amount will make about 10 croquettes). Beat the remaining egg with the milk and oil. Dip the croquettes into the flour, then into the egg mixture and the breadcrumbs. Put on to a tray or baking sheet and open freeze. Pack into a rigid container with foil or clingfilm between the layers, and store.

TO SERVE
Fry the frozen croquettes in deep fat until golden. Drain well before serving.
HIGH QUALITY STORAGE LIFE   2 months

Sweet and Sour Red Cabbage

15g/½ oz butter
1 medium onion
15ml/1 tablespoon brown
    sugar
15ml/1 tablespoon cider
    vinegar
900g/2 lb red cabbage
salt and pepper
150ml/¼ pint cider
2 small tart apples

Melt the butter and fry the sliced onion until soft. Add the sugar, vinegar and the cabbage which has been finely shredded. Add salt and pepper and the cider and cover tightly. Simmer for 1 hour. Peel and core the apples and cut them into slices. Stir into the cabbage and continue cooking for 1 hour. Pack into a rigid container and freeze.

TO SERVE
Heat gently in a double saucepan, or in a moderate oven, and serve with pork, bacon or goose.
HIGH QUALITY STORAGE LIFE   2 months

Baked Leeks

16 large or 24 small leeks
water or chicken stock
75ml/5 tablespoons butter
30ml/2 tablespoons double
    cream
salt and black pepper

FOR SERVING
grated cheese
bacon rasher

Put the leeks in a large pan. Add water or chicken stock barely to cover, and simmer with lid on for 5 minutes. Drain leeks and transfer to a foil freezer dish. Add butter and cream and bake at 180°C/350°F/Gas 4, turning occasionally, for 10 minutes. Season with salt and pepper to taste. Cool, cover and freeze.

TO SERVE
Uncover, sprinkle with grated cheese, cover with a rasher of bacon and heat at 180°C/350°F/Gas 4 for 35 minutes.
HIGH QUALITY STORAGE LIFE   1 month

Spinach Flan

450g/1 lb shortcrust pastry
675g/1½ lb spinach
50g/2 oz butter
2 eggs
225g/8 oz full fat soft cream
    cheese
50g/2 oz grated Parmesan
    cheese
salt and pepper
a pinch of ground nutmeg

Roll out the pastry to line a flan ring and bake blind in a fairly hot oven, 200°C/400°F/Gas 6, for 15 minutes. Wash the spinach very well and then put into a pan with the butter. Cover and cook for about 8 minutes until soft. Drain well and press out excess moisture. Put into a bowl and add the eggs and cream cheese beaten together. Stir in the grated Parmesan cheese, salt, pepper and nutmeg. Put into the pastry case. Cool. Open freeze, then wrap in foil or polythene, or put in a box, and store.

TO SERVE
Unwrap and return the flan to the flan ring. Bake from frozen in a very hot oven, 230°C/450°F/Gas 8, for 15 minutes, and then in a fairly hot oven, 190°C/375°F/Gas 5, for 25 minutes. Leave to stand for 5 minutes before removing the flan ring. Serve hot or cold.
HIGH QUALITY STORAGE LIFE   1 month

Mushroom Flan

225g/8 oz shortcrust pastry
1 medium onion
15g/½ oz butter
225g/8 oz button
    mushrooms
15ml/1 tablespoon lemon
    juice
2 eggs
150ml/¼ pint single cream
salt and pepper
5ml/1 teaspoon chopped
    fresh parsley

Roll out the pastry to line a flan ring and bake blind in a fairly hot oven, 200°C/400°F/Gas 6, for 15 minutes. Chop the onion finely and cook in the butter until soft and golden. Stir in the chopped mushrooms and lemon juice, and cook for 2 minutes. Cool. Beat together the eggs and cream and then stir in the mushrooms and onion. Season well and add the parsley. Pour into the pastry base. Bake in a fairly hot oven, 200°C/400°F/Gas 6, for 40 minutes. Cool. Open freeze, then wrap in foil or polythene, or put into a box, and store.

TO SERVE
Unwrap and reheat from frozen in a moderate oven, 180°C/350°F/Gas 4, for 45 minutes.
HIGH QUALITY STORAGE LIFE   2 months

Quiche Lorraine

225g/8oz shortcrust pastry
15g/½ oz butter
1 small onion
25g/1 oz streaky bacon
1 egg
1 egg yolk
50g/2 oz grated Cheddar
    cheese
150ml/¼ pint creamy milk
salt and pepper

Roll out the pastry to line a flan ring. Bake the pastry blind in a fairly hot oven, 200°C/400°F/Gas 6, for 15 minutes. Melt the butter and cook the chopped onion and bacon until golden. Put into the pastry case. Lightly beat together the egg, egg yolk, cheese and milk. Season with pepper and a little salt, if the bacon is not very salty. Pour into the pastry case. Bake in a fairly hot oven, 190°C/375°F/Gas 5, for 30 minutes. Cool. Open freeze, then wrap in foil or polythene, or put into a box, and store.

TO SERVE
Thaw at room temperature to serve cold. If preferred hot, unwrap and heat in a moderate oven, 180°C/350°F/Gas 4, for 20 minutes.
HIGH QUALITY STORAGE LIFE   2 months

Pizza with Anchovies and Olives

8g/¼ oz fresh yeast *or*
   5ml/1 teaspoon dried
   yeast
150ml/¼ pint warm water
8g/¼ oz lard
225g/8 oz strong plain flour
   (white *or* white and
   brown mixed)
5ml/1 teaspoon salt
olive oil

FILLING
olive oil
350g/12 oz cheese
450g/1 lb sliced *or* canned
   tomatoes
pepper
5ml/1 teaspoon fresh
   thyme, oregano,
   marjoram *or* basil

FOR SERVING
anchovy fillets
black olives

Blend the fresh yeast into the warm water, or reconstitute the dried yeast as directed on the packet. Leave for 10 minutes. Rub the fat into the flour and salt. Mix the yeast liquid into the dry ingredients and work to a firm dough, adding extra flour if needed, until the dough leaves the bowl clean. Turn it on to a lightly floured surface and knead until it feels smooth and elastic. Leave the dough to rise in a lightly greased polythene bag until doubled in size.

Turn the risen dough on to a board. Flatten with the knuckles or a rolling-pin to a long strip. Brush with oil and roll up like a Swiss roll. Repeat this 3 times in all. Divide the dough into 4 pizzas if making individual pizzas, and roll each piece into a flat circle to fit 17.5cm/7 inch foil plates, or roll out the dough to fit 1 large foil plate.

To make the filling, brush the dough with olive oil and cover with alternate layers of cheese, tomato and seasoning, finishing with a layer of cheese. Bake in the top shelf of a very hot oven, 230°C/450°F/Gas 8, for 25–30 minutes. Cool, then wrap in foil and freeze.

TO SERVE
Unwrap and thaw at room temperature for 1 hour. Garnish with anchovy fillets and olives, and heat in a fairly hot oven, 190°C/375°F/Gas 5, for 25 minutes.
HIGH QUALITY STORAGE LIFE   2 months

Quick Mushroom Pizza

350g/12 oz self-raising flour
5ml/1 teaspoon salt
150ml/¼ pint cooking oil
90ml/6 tablespoons water
175g/6 oz lean bacon
175g/6 oz onions
450g/1 lb mushrooms
pepper
a pinch of rosemary
125g/4 oz grated Gruyère
   cheese
25g/1 oz grated Parmesan
   cheese

Mix the flour and salt and mix with the oil and water to make a soft dough. Divide into 2 pieces and roll to make a soft dough, then roll out into large thin rounds. Bake in a very hot oven, 230°C/450°F/Gas 8 for 15 minutes and cool. Put the chopped bacon into a pan and heat gently until the fat runs. Stir in the chopped onions and continue cooking until the onions are soft and golden. Add the chopped mushrooms and cook until they are just soft. Season with pepper and rosemary and spread the mixture on the 2 baked circles. Top with a thick crust of grated cheese. Cool, then wrap in foil or polythene to freeze.

TO SERVE
Unwrap and cover loosely with foil. Bake from frozen in a moderate oven, 180°C/350°F/Gas 4, for 45 minutes. Remove the foil and continue heating for 10 minutes.
HIGH QUALITY STORAGE LIFE   1 month

Rice

Rice is a useful item for the freezer, to be combined with sauces, or to serve with other freezer dishes. It should be slightly undercooked in boiling salted water. After thorough draining it should be cooled under cold running water in a sieve, then shaken as dry as possible, packed into polythene bags and frozen.

To serve, the rice is put into a pan of boiling water until just tender, the time depending on the state in which it has been frozen. Rice can also be reheated in a frying pan with a little melted butter. It should not, however, be frozen in liquid such as soup, as it then becomes slushy; it is better to freeze the rice separately and add it to the soup when reheating.

Pasta

Pasta such as spaghetti and macaroni may be successfully frozen to be used with a variety of sauces. Pasta shapes may be frozen to use with soup, but they should not be frozen in liquid as they become slushy, and so are most conveniently added to soup during the reheating period.

Pasta should be slightly undercooked in boiling salted water. After thorough draining, it should be cooled under cold running water in a sieve, then shaken as dry as possible, packed into polythene bags, and frozen.

To serve, the pasta is put into a pan of boiling water and brought back to the boil, then simmered until just tender; the time depends on the state in which it has been frozen.

Macaroni Cheese

225g/8 oz macaroni
50g/2 oz butter
50g/2 oz plain flour
750ml/1¼ pints milk
225g/8 oz grated Cheddar
  cheese
salt and pepper

FOR SERVING
rashers of bacon
hard-boiled egg slices

Cook the macaroni as directed on the packet and drain well. Melt the butter and work in the flour. Cook for 1 minute and work in the milk. Stir over a gentle heat until the sauce is smooth and creamy. Over a very slow heat, stir in the grated cheese and seasoning. Mix the macaroni and cheese sauce, then cool. Pack into a foil container and cover with a lid to freeze. If liked, some chopped cooked ham or bacon, chopped cooked onions or mushrooms can be added to the macaroni cheese before freezing.

TO SERVE
Remove the lid, cover the container with foil and heat in a fairly hot oven, 200°C/400°F/Gas 6, for 1 hour, removing the foil for the last 15 minutes to brown the top. Garnish with bacon rashers and sliced hard-boiled eggs.
HIGH QUALITY STORAGE LIFE   1 month

Gnocchi

1 medium onion
1 bay leaf
600ml/1 pint milk
75g/3 oz semolina
salt and pepper
40g/1½ oz grated Cheddar
   cheese
15g/½ oz butter
5ml/1 teaspoon made
   mustard
50g/2 oz melted butter
50g/2 oz grated Cheddar
   cheese

Put the onion into a pan with the bay leaf and milk. Cover, and bring slowly to the boil. Remove from the heat and leave to stand for 5 minutes, then take out the onion and bay leaf. Stir in the semolina and mix well. Add salt and pepper and simmer for 15 minutes until creamy. Put to one side, stir in the cheese, butter and mustard, and spread out the mixture on a tin or plate about 2cm/¾ inch thick. Leave until cold and set, then cut into 5cm/ 2 inch squares. Pack in layers in a foil tray, brushing each layer with melted butter and sprinkling with grated cheese. Cover and freeze.

TO SERVE
Thaw at room temperature for 1 hour, then uncover and bake in a moderate oven, 180°C/350°F/Gas 4, for 45 minutes until golden and crisp.
HIGH QUALITY STORAGE LIFE   2 months

Spinach Noodles with Cheese

450g/1 lb noodles
1 large onion
1 garlic clove
15g/½ oz butter
225g/8 oz lean bacon
450g/1 lb spinach
300ml/½ pint soured cream
salt and pepper
a pinch of nutmeg
200g/7 oz Gruyère cheese

Cook the noodles in boiling water for 6–8 minutes until tender, then drain thoroughly. Chop the onion finely, crush the garlic clove and cook in the butter until soft and golden. Chop the bacon and cook with the onion until soft. Stir the onion and bacon into the noodles and arrange in a freezer-to-table container. Wash the spinach very well and put into a saucepan without any water. Cook over gentle heat until the spinach is soft. Drain very thoroughly and press out any liquid. Mash the spinach with a potato masher and then work in the soured cream, salt, pepper and nutmeg. Arrange in the centre of the noodles. Cool completely and cover with thin slices of cheese. Cover with foil or a lid to freeze.

TO SERVE
Remove the lid and cover the dish with foil. Heat in a moderate oven, 180°C/350°F/Gas 4, for 40 minutes. Remove the foil and continue cooking for 15 minutes until the cheese has melted.
HIGH QUALITY STORAGE LIFE   1 month

Pasta should be slightly undercooked when being prepared for freezing

put on to sandwich plates in their frozen state. Chopped frozen herbs and herb butter can also be used to add to soups or sauces.

Julienne Vegetables

Root vegetables such as carrots and turnips can be cut in matchstick slices and frozen in small bags. It is best to blanch them for long-term storage, but this is not necessary if they are to be frozen for less than 1 month. They can be added to soup just before serving.

Tomato Sauce

25g/1 oz butter
1 small onion
1 small carrot
450g/1 lb ripe tomatoes
25g/1 oz ham
600ml/1 pint stock
a sprig of parsley
a sprig of thyme
1 bay leaf
25g/1 oz cornflour

Melt the butter and fry the sliced onion and carrot until soft and golden. Add the sliced tomatoes, chopped ham, stock and herbs and simmer for 30 minutes. Put through a sieve, and return to a clean saucepan. Mix the cornflour with a little water and stir into the sauce. Simmer for 5 minutes, stirring well. Cool and pack in a rigid container to freeze.

TO SERVE
Reheat in a double saucepan or a bowl over hot water, stirring gently.
HIGH QUALITY STORAGE LIFE   12 months

Maître d'Hôtel Butter

50g/2 oz butter
10ml/2 teaspoons lemon
   juice
10ml/2 teaspoons chopped
   parsley
salt and pepper

Cream the butter and work in the other ingredients. Form the butter into a cylinder shape and wrap in foil or polythene, then freeze.

TO SERVE
Unwrap the butter and cut the cylinder in slices to form round pats. Serve on grilled meat or fish, or vegetables.
HIGH QUALITY STORAGE LIFE   2 months

Lemon Sauce

300ml/½ pint water
juice and rind of 1 lemon
25g/1 oz cornflour
30ml/2 tablespoons sugar
25g/1 oz butter

Boil the water with the lemon juice and rind. Mix the cornflour with a little cold water and then add to the hot liquid together with the sugar. Stir over a gentle heat until the sauce is smooth. Cool and stir in the butter. Pack in a rigid container, leaving headspace, and freeze.

TO SERVE
Heat gently in a double saucepan to serve with puddings.
HIGH QUALITY STORAGE LIFE   2 months

Cranberry Sauce

350/12 oz sugar
450ml/¾ pint water
450g/1 lb cranberries

Dissolve the sugar in the water over a gentle heat, add the cranberries and cook gently for 15 minutes until the cranberries pop. Cool. Pack in small waxed containers to freeze.

TO SERVE
Thaw at room temperature for 3 hours.
HIGH QUALITY STORAGE LIFE   12 months

Gooseberry Sauce

450g/1 lb gooseberries
30ml/2 tablespoons water
25g/1 oz butter
50g/2 oz sugar

Wash the gooseberries but do not top and tail them. Put them into a pan with the water and butter, cover and cook for 15 minutes on a low heat. When the berries are soft, put through a sieve, extracting as much liquid as possible. Reheat the purée with the sugar, stirring until it has dissolved. Cool and pack in small containers to freeze.

TO SERVE
Reheat gently and use with fish, or with ices or steamed puddings.
HIGH QUALITY STORAGE LIFE   2 months

Spiced Apple Sauce

450g/1 lb cooking apples
125g/4 oz sugar
1.25ml/¼ teaspoon
  cinnamon
1.25ml/¼ teaspoon nutmeg
30ml/2 tablespoons water

Peel and core the apples and cut them into quarters. Put into a pan with the sugar, spices and water. Simmer for 25 minutes until the apples are soft. Beat lightly and cool. Pack into a rigid container and freeze.

TO SERVE
Heat very gently, stirring well, and serve with fruit puddings.
HIGH QUALITY STORAGE LIFE   2 months

Strawberry Sauce

450g/1 lb strawberries
175g/6 oz caster sugar
juice of 2 lemons

Sieve the fruit. Stir in sugar and strained lemon juice and continue stirring until the sugar has dissolved. Pack into rigid containers and freeze.

TO SERVE
Thaw in refrigerator and serve cold over ice cream, cakes or puddings.
HIGH QUALITY STORAGE LIFE   12 months

Brandy Butter

50g/2 oz butter
50g/2 oz icing sugar
30ml/2 tablespoons brandy

Cream the butter and sugar and work in the brandy. Pack in small rigid containers, pressing down well, and freeze.

TO SERVE
Thaw in refrigerator for 1 hour before serving with puddings or mince pies.
HIGH QUALITY STORAGE LIFE   12 months

Brandy Butter

Chocolate Sauce

300ml/½ pint milk
15g/½ oz cornflour
15g/½ oz cocoa
25g/1 oz sugar

Heat the milk to boiling point. Mix the cornflour and cocoa with a little water. Add a little of the hot milk, blend well, and add to the remaining milk. Add the sugar and cook for 3 minutes, stirring well, until the sauce is thick. Cool and pack into a rigid container, leaving headspace, and freeze.

TO SERVE
Reheat gently in a double saucepan to serve over ice cream or puddings.
HIGH QUALITY STORAGE LIFE   2 months

Basic Poultry Stuffing

1 egg
50g/2 oz shredded suet
125g/4 oz fresh
   breadcrumbs
10ml/2 teaspoons chopped
   parsley
5ml/1 teaspoon chopped
   thyme
5ml/1 teaspoon grated
   lemon rind
salt and pepper

Mix all the ingredients, beginning with the beaten egg. Pack into a polythene bag for freezer storage.

TO SERVE
Thaw in refrigerator for 2 hours and then stuff the bird. This stuffing may also be used for whole fish such as haddock, cod or mackerel.
HIGH QUALITY STORAGE LIFE   1 month

Chestnut Stuffing

450g/1 lb chestnuts
milk
50g/2 oz fresh white
   breadcrumbs
25g/1 oz melted butter
10ml/2 teaspoons fresh
   mixed herbs
2 eggs
salt and pepper
a pinch of mustard powder

Peel the chestnuts, then simmer in a little milk until tender. Sieve and mix with breadcrumbs, butter, herbs and eggs. Add salt and pepper and a pinch of dry mustard. Pack in cartons or polythene bags to freeze.

TO SERVE
Thaw in refrigerator for 12 hours before stuffing the bird.
HIGH QUALITY STORAGE LIFE   1 month

PUDDINGS, DESSERTS AND ICES

Cherry Crumble

675g/1½ lb stoned cherries
75ml/5 tablespoons water
25g/1 oz caster sugar
50g/2 oz butter
125g/4 oz self-raising flour
50g/2 oz soft brown sugar
a pinch of ground mixed
    spice

Put the cherries, water and caster sugar into a freezer-proof pie dish. Mix the butter into flour and rub until the mixture is like fine breadcrumbs. Stir in the brown sugar and spice and mix thoroughly. Sprinkle on top of the cherries. Bake in a fairly hot oven, 190°C/375°F/Gas 5, for 45 minutes until the top is golden. Cool and cover with foil or polythene to freeze. The crumble may be frozen uncooked. But as it is good to eat cold, it is more useful to store it ready-cooked.

TO SERVE
Thaw at room temperature for 4 hours to eat cold with cream, or reheat in a moderate oven, 180°C/350°F/Gas 4, for 45 minutes to serve hot with custard.

HIGH QUALITY STORAGE LIFE   2 months

Gooseberry Crumb Tart

225g/8oz shortcrust pastry
450g/1 lb gooseberries
125g/4 oz soft breadcrumbs
45ml/3 tablespoons melted
    butter
3 eggs
50g/2 oz sugar

FOR SERVING
caster sugar

Line a foil pie plate with the pastry. Cook the gooseberries in just enough water to cover until they are soft, and sweeten to taste. Rub through a sieve and mix with the breadcrumbs, butter, eggs and sugar. Pour into the pastry case and bake in a moderate oven, 180°C/350°F/Gas 4, for 40 minutes. Cool, cover and freeze.

TO SERVE
Thaw at room temperature for 3 hours to serve cold, and sprinkle with caster sugar. To serve hot, heat in a moderate oven, 180°C/350°F/Gas 4, for 30 minutes, and sprinkle with caster sugar.

HIGH QUALITY STORAGE LIFE   2 months

Peach Pie

225g/8oz puff pastry
450g/1 lb fresh *or* canned
    peach halves
3 eggs
125g/4 oz icing sugar
125g/4 oz ground almonds

Line a deep foil pie plate with the pastry. Arrange the peach halves on this, cut side down. Beat the eggs well and work in the icing sugar and almonds. Pour over the peaches. bake in a fairly hot oven, 190°C/375°F/Gas 5, for 35 minutes. Cool, wrap in foil or polythene and freeze.

TO SERVE
Heat in a moderate oven, 180°C/350°F/Gas 4, for 30 minutes.

HIGH QUALITY STORAGE LIFE   2 months

Pancakes

125g/4 oz plain flour
1.25ml/¼ teaspoon salt
1 egg
1 egg yolk
300ml/½ pint milk
15ml/1 tablespoon oil *or*
    melted butter

Sift the flour and salt and mix in the egg and egg yolk with a little milk. Work together until creamy, and gradually add the remaining milk, beating to a smooth batter. Fold in the oil or melted butter. Fry large thin pancakes. When cool, pack in layers separated by clingfilm, then wrap in foil or a polythene bag to freeze.

TO SERVE
Separate the pancakes, put on a baking sheet and cover with foil. Heat in a cool oven, 150°C/300°F/Gas 2, and fill with jam or fruit, or serve with sugar and lemon juice. The pancakes may also be thawed at room temperature and filled with a savoury filling, then covered with a cheese, mushroom or tomato sauce for reheating.
HIGH QUALITY STORAGE LIFE   2 months

Spiced Orange Pudding

75g/3 oz butter
50g/2 oz soft brown sugar
grated rind of 1 orange
75g/3 oz black treacle
1 egg
175g/6 oz self-raising flour
5ml/1 teaspoon ground
    cinnamon
40g/1½ oz chopped glacé
    cherries
50g/2 oz seedless raisins

FOR SERVING
juice of 2 oranges
150ml/¼ pint water
15ml/1 tablespoon
    cornflour
sugar

Cream the butter, sugar and orange rind until light and fluffy, and beat in the treacle. Whisk the egg and add gradually, and stir in the sifted flour and cinnamon. Add the cherries and raisins, and put into a greased pudding basin. Cover with foil and steam for 1½ hours. Cool, cover and freeze.

TO SERVE
Steam for 1 hour and serve with orange sauce made by cooking the oranges, water and cornflour, and sweetening to taste.
HIGH QUALITY STORAGE LIFE   1 month

Chocolate Whisky Gâteau

16 sponge fingers
125g/4 oz butter
125g/4 oz caster sugar
3 eggs
125g/4 oz plain chocolate
30ml/2 tablespoons whisky

Grease a loose-bottomed cake tin very lightly with butter and put the sponge fingers round the edge so that they fit close together. Cream the butter and sugar, and gradually work in the egg yolks. Melt the chocolate over hot water and gradually whip it into the butter mixture, together with the whisky. Whisk the egg whites until they are stiff and dry, and fold them into the chocolate mixture. Pour into the tin and chill. Open freeze, then remove from the tin and wrap in foil or polythene to store.

TO SERVE
Thaw in refrigerator for 2 hours.
HIGH QUALITY STORAGE LIFE   1 month

Pancakes

Citrus Soufflé

1 envelope *or* 15ml/
    1 tablespoon gelatine
75ml/3 fl oz hot water
175g/ 6 oz caster sugar
3 eggs
30ml/2 tablespoons orange
    juice
grated rind and juice of 1
    lemon
300ml/½ pint double cream
50g/2 oz chopped nuts

Prepare the soufflé dish by cutting a collar of greaseproof paper long enough to go around the outside of the dish with about 7.5cm/3 inches overlap. Fold in half lengthways and secure into position so that the collar stands above the top of the dish by about 5cm/2 inches. Dissolve the gelatine in the hot water. Cool. Whisk the sugar and egg yolks until thick and light in colour. Add the juices and rind and continue whisking for another minute. Stir in the gelatine mixture, and set aside to thicken slightly. Whip the cream and fold gently into the mixture. Turn into the soufflé dish. Stand in a cool place until set. Remove the paper collar. Decorate the sides with chopped nuts. Wrap the sides with clingfilm and open freeze. Wrap in foil or polythene and store.

TO SERVE
Remove the outer wrapping and place a piece of clingfilm on the top. When thawed, carefully remove the top film and, just before serving, remove the piece around the sides.
HIGH QUALITY STORAGE LIFE   1 month

Apple and Rhubarb Fool

450g/1 lb rhubarb
450g/1 lb apples
125g/4 oz granulated sugar
60ml/4 tablespoons water

Cut the rhubarb into 2.5cm/1 inch pieces. Put the sliced apple, rhubarb, sugar and water in a saucepan, cover and cook very gently until soft. Mix together well. Liquidize or sieve into a smooth purée. Pack in a rigid container and freeze.

TO SERVE
Thaw in refrigerator for 3 hours, and serve with cream.
HIGH QUALITY STORAGE LIFE   12 months

Charlotte Marsala

225g/8 oz sponge fingers
Marsala
150g/5 oz butter
150g/5 oz icing sugar
5 egg yolks
150g/5 oz walnuts

FOR SERVING
whipped cream

Dip the sponge fingers quickly into the Marsala and arrange them close together round the sides and on the bottom of a greased loose-bottomed cake tin. Cream the butter and work in the sugar and egg yolks until the mixture is light and fluffy. Add the chopped walnuts and press the mixture lightly into the centre of the tin. Cover and freeze until firm. Remove from the tin and wrap in foil or polythene for storage.

TO SERVE
Thaw at room temperature for 3 hours, and decorate with whipped cream.
HIGH QUALITY STORAGE LIFE   2 months

Rum Babas

125g/4 oz plain flour
a pinch of salt
8g/¼ oz fresh yeast *or*
    5ml/1 teaspoon dried
    yeast
120ml/8 tablespoons warm
    milk
1 egg
40g/1½ oz melted butter
25g/1 oz raisins

SYRUP
50g/2 oz sugar
150ml/¼ pint water
a squeeze of lemon juice
30ml//2 tablespoons rum

FOR SERVING
rum
whipped cream

Sift the flour and salt into a warm bowl. Blend the fresh yeast in the warm milk or reconstitute the dried yeast as directed on the packet. Mix with the flour and leave in a warm place for 20 minutes until the surface is covered with bubbles. Gradually add the egg, melted butter and raisins, and knead well for 10 minutes. Put the dough into individual greased and dusted pudding moulds and leave in a warm place until it reaches the top of the moulds. Bake in a very hot oven, 230°C/450°F/Gas 8, for 15 minutes. Reduce to fairly hot, 190°C/375°F/Gas 5, and cook for 15 minutes.

To make the syrup, dissolve the sugar in the water and lemon juice and boil for 2 minutes. Cool and add the rum. Turn out the babas on a rack and soak with the rum syrup while still hot. Baste with the syrup until it is all absorbed. Pack into individual rigid containers and freeze.

TO SERVE
Thaw at room temperature for 3 hours without wrappings. Sprinkle with a little rum, and fill with whipped cream.
HIGH QUALITY STORAGE LIFE   2 months

Lemon Flummery

300ml/½ pint water
20g/¾ oz butter
1 lemon
25g/1 oz plain flour
125g/4 oz caster sugar
2 eggs

FOR SERVING
chopped nuts *or* crushed
    digestive biscuits

Boil together the water, butter and grated rind of the lemon. Mix the flour and sugar in a bowl and pour on the hot liquid, whisking well. Return to the pan and whisk in the egg yolks. Bring slowly to the boil, and cook gently for 10 minutes. Add the juice of the lemon to the pan, and fold in the stiffly whisked egg whites. Pour into a freezer-proof serving dish. Chill until set, then wrap in foil or polythene, and freeze.

TO SERVE
Thaw in refrigerator for 3 hours. Sprinkle the top with chopped nuts or crushed biscuits.
HIGH QUALITY STORAGE LIFE   1 month

Summer Fruit Bowl

450g/1 lb gooseberries
125g/4 oz redcurrants
150ml/¼ pint water
175g/6 oz caster sugar
125g/4 oz raspberries
125g/4 oz blackberries

Put the gooseberries and redcurrants in the water with the sugar and bring slowly to the boil. Simmer very gently for 5 minutes without breaking the fruit. Cool and stir in the raspberries and blackberries. Pack in waxed or rigid containers and freeze.

TO SERVE
Thaw in refrigerator for 3 hours and serve with cream.
HIGH QUALITY STORAGE LIFE   12 months

Fruit Flan

175g/6 oz plain flour
a pinch of salt
15ml/1 tablespoon icing
   sugar
75g/3 oz butter
2 egg yolks
15ml/1 tablespoon iced
   water

FOR SERVING
fruit
apricot jam *or* redcurrant
   jelly

Sift the flour, salt and sugar on to a board. Make a well in the centre and put in the butter cut into small pieces. Add the egg yolks and work together with a palette knife until the mixture is like breadcrumbs. Sprinkle in the water and knead the dough on a lightly floured board until smooth. Chill in the refrigerator for 30 minutes and then roll out carefully to fit a foil flan tin. Bake blind in a hot oven, 220°C/425°F/Gas 7, for 15 minutes, then continue baking for about 10 minutes until the pastry is crisp and golden. Cool and wrap in foil to freeze.

TO SERVE
Unwrap and thaw on a serving plate at room temperature for 1 hour. Arrange fruit in the flan case and brush thickly with hot sieved apricot jam or redcurrant jelly.
HIGH QUALITY STORAGE LIFE   2 months

Fruit Flan

Lemon Cheesecake

Lemon Cheesecake

125g/4 oz finely crushed
   digestive biscuit crumbs
75g/3 oz melted margarine
25g/1 oz soft brown sugar
225g/8 oz full fat soft cream
   cheese
75g/3 oz caster sugar
2 eggs
150g/5 oz lemon yoghurt
   (see **Note**)
juice and rind of ½ lemon
15g/½ oz gelatine
60ml/4 tablespoons water
150ml/¼ pint double cream

FOR SERVING
lemon twists
melted chocolate

Put the crumbs in a basin and stir in the melted margarine mixed with the brown sugar. Press into the base of a greased loose-bottomed cake tin, and leave in a cold place for a few minutes until firm.

Cream the cheese and caster sugar until smooth and gradually work in the egg yolks, yoghurt, lemon rind and juice. Dissolve the gelatine in water and heat gently until syrupy. Cool slightly and add to the cheese mixture. Whip the cream lightly and fold into the mixture. Whisk the egg whites to soft peaks and fold into the mixture. Pour over the base and chill until firm.

Remove from the tin, leaving the cheesecake on the metal base. Open freeze and when firm, turn upside-down on to a piece of foil. Ease away the metal base of the cake tin. Wrap the foil round the cheesecake, put in a box and store.

Note If lemon yoghurt is not available, use natural yoghurt and add the juice and rind of 1 lemon.

TO SERVE
Thaw in refrigerator without wrappings for 6 hours. Decorate with lemon twists and melted chocolate.

HIGH QUALITY STORAGE LIFE   1 month

115

Baked Cheesecake

50g/2 oz crushed digestive biscuit crumbs
450g/1 lb cottage cheese
5ml/1 teaspoon lemon juice
5ml/1 teaspoon grated orange rind
15ml/1 tablespoon cornflour
30ml/2 tablespoons double cream
2 eggs
125g/4 oz caster sugar

Butter the sides and line the base of a loose-bottomed cake tin with buttered paper. Sprinkle with biscuit crumbs. Sieve the cottage cheese and mix with the lemon juice, orange rind and cornflour. Whip the cream and stir in. Beat the egg yolks until thick, then stir into the cheese mixture. Beat the egg whites until stiff and beat in half the sugar, then stir in the remaining sugar. Fold into the cheese mixture and put into the baking tin. Bake in a moderate oven, 180°C/350°F/Gas 4, for 1 hour and leave to cool in the oven. Remove from the tin. Open freeze and wrap in foil, and then in a box to avoid crushing.

TO SERVE
Thaw in refrigerator for 8 hours.
HIGH QUALITY STORAGE LIFE   1 month

Fresh Fruit Mousse

150ml/¼ pint fruit purée
25g/1 oz caster sugar
150ml/¼ pint double cream
2 egg whites
juice of ½ lemon

Mix the fruit purée and sugar. Whip the cream lightly, and whisk the egg whites until stiff. Add lemon juice to the fruit, then fold in the cream and egg whites. Pack in a serving dish, then in foil or polythene to freeze.

TO SERVE
Thaw in refrigerator for 2 hours.
HIGH QUALITY STORAGE LIFE   1 month

Basic Custard Ice

300ml/½ pint milk
1 vanilla pod
2 egg yolks
50g/2 oz sugar
a pinch of salt
150ml/¼ pint double cream

Scald the milk with the vanilla pod, remove the pod and pour the milk on to the egg yolks which have been lightly beaten with sugar and salt. Cook in a double boiler until the mixture coats the back of a spoon. Cool and strain. Stir in the cream. Pour into freezing trays and beat twice during a total freezing time of 3 hours. Pack into containers, cover and freeze.

HIGH QUALITY STORAGE LIFE   3 months

Basic Cream Ice

600ml/1 pint thin cream
1 vanilla pod
75g/3 oz sugar
a pinch of salt

Heat the cream with the vanilla pod, remove from the heat, stir in the sugar and salt, and cool. Remove the vanilla pod and freeze the mixture to a mush. Beat well in a chilled bowl, and continue freezing for a total of 2 hours. Pack into containers, cover and freeze.

HIGH QUALITY STORAGE LIFE   3 months

Basic Gelatine Ice

450ml/¾ pint creamy milk
1 vanilla pod
10ml/2 teaspoons gelatine
30ml/2 tablespoons water
75g/3 oz sugar
a pinch of salt

Heat 150ml/¼ pint milk with the vanilla pod to boiling point. Soak the gelatine in the water, and heat the bowl standing in hot water until the gelatine is syrupy. Pour the warm milk on the gelatine, stir in the sugar and salt, and add the remaining milk. Remove the vanilla pod. Put into a freezing tray and beat twice during 3 hours freezing time. Pack into containers, cover and freeze.

Note This mixture is particularly good with added flavourings.

HIGH QUALITY STORAGE LIFE   3 months

Rich Ice Cream

2 eggs
75g/3 oz caster sugar
450ml/¾ pint milk
10ml/2 teaspoons gelatine
30ml/2 tablespoons hot
    water
300ml/½ pint double cream
5ml/1 teaspoon vanilla
    essence

Whisk the eggs with the sugar and milk in a basin over a pan of hot water until the mixture thickens. Cool. Dissolve the gelatine in the hot water. Cool. Add to the custard. Whip the cream and carefully fold into the mixture. Add the vanilla essence. Pour into a freezing tray and freeze until firm around the edges. Turn into a bowl. Beat until smooth. Return to the tray and freeze until required. Pack into a rigid container, cover and freeze.

HIGH QUALITY STORAGE LIFE   3 months

Chocolate Ice Cream

300ml/½ pint milk
2 egg yolks
125g/4 oz sugar
125g/4 oz plain chocolate
5ml/1 teaspoon instant
    coffee powder
150ml/¼ pint double cream

Bring the milk almost to boiling point. Beat the egg yolks and sugar until creamy, and pour on the milk, beating well. Return the mixture to the saucepan and stir over a very low heat until the mixture forms a creamy custard. Put the chocolate and coffee powder into a bowl over hot water and heat until melted. Add this chocolate mixture to the custard and cool, stirring occasionally. Whip the cream to soft peaks and fold into the chocolate mixture. Put into a freezing tray and beat once half-way through a total freezing time of 3 hours.

HIGH QUALITY STORAGE LIFE   3 months

Brown Bread Ice Cream

Brown Bread Ice Cream

175g/6 oz fresh wholemeal
    bread (no crusts)
600ml/1 pint double cream
225g/8 oz sugar
60ml/4 tablespoons water

Cut the bread in slices and put in a very cool oven, 120°C/250°F/Gas ½, until dry. Break into coarse crumbs. Whip the cream and mix in 175g/6 oz sugar. Put the cream into a freezing tray, cover with foil and freeze for 1 hour. Melt the remaining sugar in the water and cool. Pour it on the breadcrumbs. Mix the breadcrumbs in syrup into the cream mixture and put into one or two freezing trays. Freeze until firm, then pack into a rigid container for storage.

HIGH QUALITY STORAGE LIFE   3 months

Raspberry Water Ice

125g/4 oz sugar
300ml/½ pint water
450g/1 lb raspberries

Put the sugar and water in a pan and boil for 5 minutes. Cool. Sieve the raspberries. Blend together with the syrup and freeze for 3 hours, whisking in a chilled bowl half-way through freezing. The ice will be improved if a stiffly whisked egg white is folded in after the ice has been whisked. Pack into a rigid container for storage.

HIGH QUALITY STORAGE LIFE   1 month

Fresh Fruit Mousse (page 116) **and** *Raspberry Water Ice*

Lemon Water Ice

225g/8 oz sugar
450ml/¾ pint water
2 lemons
1.25ml/¼ teaspoon ground
    ginger
salt

Combine the sugar and water in a saucepan, bring to the boil, and boil for 5 minutes. Grate the rind of 1 lemon and add the juice of both lemons, together with the ground ginger and a pinch of salt. Gradually pour in the hot syrup until well blended. Cool and pour into a freezing tray, and freeze for 3 hours, stirring occasionally. Pack into a rigid container for storage.

HIGH QUALITY STORAGE LIFE   1 month

Orange Sorbet

10ml/2 teaspoons gelatine
300ml/½ pint water
175g/6 oz sugar
5ml/1 teaspoon grated
    lemon rind
5ml/1 teaspoon grated
    orange rind
300ml/½ pint orange juice
60ml/4 tablespoons lemon
    juice
2 egg whites

Soak the gelatine in a little of the water and boil the rest of the water and sugar for 10 minutes to form a syrup. Stir the gelatine into the syrup and cool. Add the rinds and juices of the orange and lemon. Whisk the egg whites until stiff but not dry and fold into the mixture. Freeze to a mush, beat once and continue freezing, allowing 3 hours total freezing time. Pack in rigid containers for storage.

Note This ice will not go completely hard.

HIGH QUALITY STORAGE LIFE   1 month

Tangerine Ice

4 large tangerines
5ml/1 teaspoon gelatine
150ml/¼ pint water
75g/3 oz sugar
5ml/1 teaspoon grated
    lemon rind
15ml/1 tablespoon lemon
    juice
1 egg white

FOR SERVING
mint leaves *or* small green
    marzipan leaves

Remove the tops of the tangerines carefully so that they will form lids. Scoop out the flesh, saving all the juice. Wash the skins carefully and dry them. Soak the gelatine in a little of the water and boil the rest of the water for 5 minutes with the sugar to form a syrup. Stir the gelatine into the syrup and leave to cool. Add the grated lemon rind and juice, and all the juice of the tangerines. Whisk the egg white into stiff peaks and fold into the gelatine mixture. Put into a freezing tray and freeze for 3 hours, beating once half-way through freezing when the ice is mushy.

    Scoop the ice into the tangerine cases and put the lids on lightly. Put into the freezer for 1 hour before serving, and decorate with mint leaves or small green marzipan leaves. For longer storage, wrap the tangerines in foil.

HIGH QUALITY STORAGE LIFE   1 month

Biscuit Tortoni

50g/2 oz toasted blanched
  almonds or macaroon
  crumbs
30ml/2 tablespoons water
65g/2½ oz caster sugar
30ml/2 tablespoons sherry
3 egg yolks
200ml/8 fl oz double cream

Grind the nuts if using. Put water and sugar in a small pan, bring to the boil and boil for 3 minutes. Put sherry and egg yolks into a bowl and gradually pour in hot syrup and blend well. Whip the cream and fold mixture into it; add the ground almonds or crumbs. Put in a freezing tray and freeze for 2 hours. Pack in rigid container for storage.

HIGH QUALITY STORAGE LIFE   1 month

Bombes

Use double-sided moulds, jelly moulds or pudding basins.

Melon Bombe
Line a mould with pistachio ice cream and freeze for 30 minutes. Fill with raspberry ice cream mixed with chocolate chips, and wrap for storage. This looks like a watermelon when cut into slices.

Raspberry Bombe
Line a mould with raspberry ice cream, freeze for 30 minutes and fill with vanilla ice cream.

Coffee Bombe
Line a mould with coffee ice cream and freeze for 30 minutes. Fill with vanilla ice cream flavoured with chopped maraschino cherries and syrup.

Three-flavoured Bombe
Line a mould with vanilla ice cream, freezing for 30 minutes. Put in a lining of praline ice cream and freeze for 30 minutes. Fill the centre with chocolate ice cream.

Tutti frutti Bombe
Line a mould with strawberry ice cream and freeze for 30 minutes. Fill with lemon sorbet mixed with very well-drained canned fruit cocktail and freeze till firm.

Raspberry-filled Bombe
Line a mould with vanilla or praline ice cream and freeze for 30 minutes. Fill with crushed raspberries beaten into whipped cream and lightly sweetened.

TO FREEZE
Wrap container in foil, seal and freeze.

TO SERVE
Turn out on to a chilled plate using a cloth wrung out in hot water. Wrap in foil and freeze for 1 hour before serving.

HIGH QUALITY STORAGE LIFE   3 months

121

Meringue Bombe

6 large meringue shells
450ml/¾ pint double cream
4 pieces preserved ginger
30ml/2 tablespoons caster
   sugar
grated rind of 1 lemon
75ml/3 fl oz kirsch

Break the meringue shells into small pieces. Whip the cream to soft peaks. Chop the ginger into small pieces. Fold the ginger, sugar, lemon rind, kirsch and broken meringue pieces into the cream. Put into a pudding basin or cake tin which has been lightly oiled, and smooth down the mixture. Cover with foil and freeze for 4 hours. Turn out of the basin or tin and wrap in foil for storage.

TO SERVE
Remove the foil and put the bombe on to a serving plate. Leave at room temperature for 10 minutes. This is delicious served with raspberries or strawberries or with a fruit sauce.
HIGH QUALITY STORAGE LIFE   1 month

Iced Zabaglione

10ml/2 teaspoons gelatine
60ml/4 tablespoons hot
   water
6 egg yolks
125g/4 oz caster sugar
150ml/¼ pint sherry
60ml/4 tablespoons brandy
10ml/2 teaspoons vanilla
   essence
300ml/½ pint double cream
5 egg whites

Dissolve the gelatine in the hot water. Cool. Beat the egg yolks and sugar until thick. Place in a basin over a pan of hot water, and add the sherry and brandy. Cook and stir until thick. Cool. Stir in the dissolved gelatine and the vanilla essence. Whip the cream and fold in carefully. Whisk the egg whites until stiff and add to the mixture. Pack in a rigid container.

TO SERVE
Remove from the freezer and allow to thaw whilst still covered. Stir lightly and spoon into individual serving dishes.
HIGH QUALITY STORAGE LIFE   1 month

Iced Zabaglione

BREADS, CAKES AND BISCUITS

Both bought and home-baked bread freezes extremely well if fresh at the time of freezing. The length of storage time varies with the type of bread. It is practical to keep one or two loaves for emergency use; baps, rolls and flavoured breads for special meals, unusual bread such as granary loaves or French sticks which may not always be obtainable from local bakers. Bread can be wrapped in heavy foil or polythene for storage, or can be frozen unwrapped for short-term storage.

Thaw bread in its wrappings at room temperature; a 675g/1½ lb loaf will take about 3 hours. Alternatively, thaw in foil in a fairly hot oven, 200°C/400°F/Gas 6, for 45 minutes. This second method will, however, make the bread go stale quickly.

Crusty bread is best 'refreshed' in a fairly hot oven, 200°C/400°F/Gas 6, for 10 minutes after thawing at room temperature.

Sliced bread can be toasted while still frozen if the slices are separated carefully with a knife before toasting.

Store white and brown breads for 4 weeks, enriched breads for 6 weeks, crisp loaves and rolls for 1 week, and Vienna loaves and rolls for 3 days.

UNCOOKED YEAST MIXTURES

Unbaked bread and buns may be frozen, but proving after freezing takes a long time, and the texture may be heavier. Unbaked dough to be frozen should be allowed to prove once, then shaped for baking, or kept in bulk if this is easier for storage. The surface should be brushed with a little olive oil or unsalted butter to prevent toughening of the crust, and a little extra sugar added to sweet mixtures.

Single loaves or a quantity of dough can be packed in foil or polythene; rolls can be packed in layers separated by clingfilm before wrapping in foil or polythene.

Thaw in a moist warm place; greater speed in thawing will give a lighter textured loaf. After shaping, prove the mixture again before baking. If the bread has been shaped before freezing, it should be proved once in a warm place before baking.

Store for 2 weeks.

Note *Fresh yeast* can be stored in the freezer for 6 months. The yeast is best bought in 225g/8 oz or 450g/1 lb packets, divided into 25g/1 oz cubes, and each cube wrapped in foil or polythene, and then a quantity of these stored in a preserving jar in the freezer. A cube of yeast will be ready for use after thawing for 30 minutes at room temperature.

SANDWICHES

Sandwiches freeze extremely well, but their storage life is limited by the type of filling. There is little point in keeping sandwiches longer than 4 weeks. Plain white bread, whole wheat, rye, pumpernickel and fruit breads can be used for frozen sandwiches, together with baps and rolls. Brown bread is good for fish fillings, and fruit bread for cheese or sweet fillings.

Preparation

Soften the butter or margarine for spreading the bread for freezer sandwiches but do not allow it to melt. Make sure that fillings are well chilled before use, and that all wrapping materials and prepared breads are ready for use before starting to assemble sandwiches.

Spread fat right to the edges of the bread to prevent fillings soaking in, and spread fillings evenly to ensure even thawing. Stack sandwiches neatly and cut them with a sharp knife, leaving in large portions (such as half-slices) with crusts on; this will prevent the sandwiches drying out and becoming mis-shapen during freezing.

Packing and freezing

Sandwiches are best packed in groups of six or eight rather than individually. Wrap them tightly in clingfilm, then in foil or polythene. This enables the outer wrapping to be removed for further use and the inner packet to be put straight into a lunch-box. If sandwiches are frozen against the freezer wall, this will result in uneven thawing, and it is best to put packages a few cm/inches from the wall of the freezer. They should be thawed in their wrappings in the refrigerator for 12 hours, or at room temperature for 4 hours.

BISCUIT DOUGH

Uncooked frozen biscuits are extremely useful, and the frozen dough will give light crisp biscuits. The best way to prepare biscuits is to freeze batches of any recipe in cylinder shapes in polythene or foil, storing them carefully to avoid dents from other packages in the freezer. The unfrozen dough should be left in its wrappings in the refrigerator for 45 minutes until it begins to soften, then cut in slices and baked. If the dough is too soft it will be difficult to cut.

Store for 2 months.

Banana Bread

Banana Bread

50g/2 oz soft margarine
3 bananas
125g/4 oz caster sugar
1 egg
90ml/6 tablespoons milk
grated rind of 1 orange
50g/2 oz walnuts
275g/10 oz plain flour
5ml/1 teaspoon baking
  powder
1.25ml/¼ teaspoon
  bicarbonate of soda
2.5 ml/½ teaspoon salt

Put the margarine into a bowl and add the bananas cut into small pieces. Mash thoroughly so that they are completely broken up. Add all the remaining ingredients, chopping the walnuts finely. Beat well and put into a loaf tin, lined on the bottom with greaseproof paper. Bake in a moderate oven, 180°C/350°F/Gas 4, for 1½ hours. Leave in the tin for 5 minutes, then turn out and cool on a wire rack. Pack in foil or polythene to freeze.

TO SERVE
Thaw in wrappings at room temperature for 3 hours.
HIGH QUALITY STORAGE LIFE   4 months

126

Croissants (page 128) **and** *Brioches (page 128)*

Brioches

225g/8 oz strong white
  flour
25g/1 oz fresh yeast *or*
  15g/½ oz dried yeast
30ml/2 tablespoons warm
  water
3 eggs
175g/6 oz melted butter
5ml/1 teaspoon salt
15g/½ oz sugar
milk

Put 50g/2 oz of the flour into a warm bowl. Blend the fresh yeast with the warm water, or reconstitute the dried yeast as directed on the packet. Mix with the flour until a ball of dough forms. Put the dough into a bowl of warm water and it will expand and form a sponge. Put the remaining flour into a bowl and beat in the eggs thoroughly. Add the butter, salt and sugar, and continue beating. Add the yeast sponge drained from the water and mix well. Cover the bowl with a damp cloth and leave to rise in a warm place for 2 hours.

Knead the dough well, cover the bowl and leave in a cool place overnight. Half fill castle pudding tins or fluted moulds with dough and top with smaller balls of dough. Leave in a warm place for 30 minutes. Brush with a little milk and bake in a very hot oven, 230°C/450°F/Gas 8, for 15 minutes. Cool and pack in polythene bags to freeze.

TO SERVE
Thaw at room temperature for 45 minutes to serve with butter.
HIGH QUALITY STORAGE LIFE   6 weeks

Croissants

150g/5 oz butter
150ml/¼ pint warm milk
5ml/1 teaspoon salt
22ml/1½ tablespoons sugar
25g/1 oz fresh yeast *or*
  15g/½ oz dried yeast
30ml/2 tablespoons warm
  water
350g/12 oz strong white
  flour
1 egg yolk beaten with a
  little milk

Put 25g/1 oz of the butter in bowl, pour on the warm milk and add the salt and sugar. Cool to lukewarm. Blend the fresh yeast with the warm water, or reconstitute the dried yeast as directed on the packet. Add to the butter mixture, then gradually add the flour to give a soft dough. Place the dough in a lightly greased polythene bag and leave for 2 hours.

Knead the dough, chill thoroughly, and roll into a rectangle. Spread the remaining butter lightly and evenly over the dough. Fold over the dough to a rectangle and roll again. Chill, roll and fold twice more at intervals of 30 minutes. Roll dough out to 1.25cm/½ inch thickness and cut into squares. Divide each square into 2 triangles, and roll each triangle up, starting at the longest edge and rolling towards the point. Bend into crescent shapes, put on a floured baking sheet, brush with beaten egg and milk, and bake in a hot oven, 220°C/425°F/Gas 7, for 15 minutes. Cool. pack into rigid containers to freeze.

TO SERVE
Heat on a baking sheet in a moderate oven, 180°C/350°F/Gas 4, for 15 minutes.
HIGH QUALITY STORAGE LIFE   6 weeks

Gingerbread

125g/4 oz self-raising flour
1.25ml/¼ teaspoon salt
5 ml/1 teaspoon ground
   ginger
50g/2 oz soft brown sugar
25g/1 oz fine oatmeal
75g/3 oz lard
75g/3 oz golden syrup
5ml/1 teaspoon warm milk
1 egg

Sift the flour, salt and ginger into a bowl. Stir in the sugar and oatmeal. Put the lard and syrup into a saucepan and heat until the lard has melted. Add the milk. Mix into the dry ingredients and beat in the egg. Beat well and pour into a greased loaf tin. Bake in a warm oven, 160°C/325°F/Gas 3, for 1¼ hours. Leave in the tin for 5 minutes, then turn out and cool on a wire rack. Pack in foil or polythene to freeze.

TO SERVE
Unwrap and thaw at room temperature for 3 hours. Serve sliced, with or without butter.
HIGH QUALITY STORAGE LIFE   1 month

Raisin and Walnut Bread

450g/1 lb plain flour
20ml/4 teaspoons baking
   powder
225g/8 oz sugar
a pinch of salt
150g/5 oz raisins
125g/4 oz chopped walnuts
2 eggs
300ml/½ pint milk
25g/1 oz melted fat

Mix together the flour, baking powder, sugar and salt, raisins and walnuts. In another bowl, beat lightly the eggs, milk and fat. Stir into the flour mixture and beat well. Pour into 2 greased and floured loaf tins and leave to stand for 30 minutes. Bake in a moderate oven, 180°C/350°F/Gas 4, for 1 hour. Leave in the tins for 5 minutes, then turn out and cool on a wire rack. Wrap in foil or polythene to freeze.

TO SERVE
Thaw at room temperature for 3 hours and serve sliced with or without butter.
HIGH QUALITY STORAGE LIFE   2 months

Cherry Madeira Cake

250g/9 oz plain flour
5ml/1 teaspoon baking
   powder
a pinch of salt
175g/6 oz caster sugar
175g/6 oz butter
3 eggs
75g/3 oz glacé cherries
milk or rum

Sift the flour with the baking powder and salt. Warm a mixing bowl and beater. Put the sugar and butter in the bowl and beat until white and fluffy. Add the eggs one at a time, beating well each time. Fold in the flour and quartered cherries. Add a little milk or rum. The mixture should shake easily from a spoon. Put in a lined cake tin and bake in a moderate oven, 180°C/350°F/Gas 4, for 1 hour and 20 minutes. Cool on a wire rack and wrap in foil to freeze.

TO SERVE
Thaw at room temperature for 3 hours.
HIGH QUALITY STORAGE LIFE   4 months

Cherry Madeira Cake
(page 129)

D1651740

Uncooked Chocolate Cake

225g/8 oz Nice biscuit
    crumbs
125g/4 oz chopped walnuts
50g/2 oz glacé cherries
75g/3 oz sultanas
125g/4 oz chopped mixed
    peel
225g/8 oz plain chocolate
175g/6 oz butter
50g/2 oz caster sugar
2 eggs
60ml/4 tablespoons sherry
    or brandy

Mix the crumbs with the nuts, quartered cherries, sultanas and peel. Put the chocolate, butter, sugar and eggs into a bowl over warm water, heat and stir gently until the chocolate has melted and the mixture is smooth. Add the sherry or brandy and stir into the biscuit crumbs and fruit. When well blended, put into a greased loose-bottomed cake tin, and chill. Remove carefully from the tin and wrap in foil or polythene to freeze.

TO SERVE
Thaw at room temperature for 3 hours and serve in small pieces as this cake is very rich.
HIGH QUALITY STORAGE LIFE   4 months

Crumble Cake

125g/4 oz sugar
225g/8 oz plain flour
175g/6 oz margarine
10ml/2 teaspoons grated
    orange *or* lemon rind

Stir the sugar into the flour and rub in the fat until the mixture looks like fine breadcrumbs. Add the grated rind. Spread in a greased shallow tin and press down lightly. Bake in a warm oven, 160°C/325°F/Gas 3, for 30 minutes. Cool in the tin and cut in slices. Pack in a rigid container to freeze.

TO SERVE
Thaw at room temperature for 3 hours. This cake is very good with fruit or ice cream.
HIGH QUALITY STORAGE LIFE   4 months

Farmhouse Apple Cake

450g/1 lb apples
6 cloves
sugar
125g/4 oz butter
125g/4 oz sugar
1 egg
225g/8 oz plain flour

Slice and cook the apples in very little water. Flavour with cloves and sweeten. Line a round foil container. Cream the butter and sugar until light and fluffy and beat in the egg. Stir in the flour until it looks like soft crumbs. Weigh off 175g/6 oz, put the remainder in the container and spread evenly. Cover the mixture with the cooked apple which must be well-drained. Cover the apple with the crumb mixture only around the edge to about 5cm/2 inches, leaving a circle in the middle. Cook in a moderate oven, 180°C/350°F/Gas 4, for 45 minutes. Cool, cover and freeze.

TO SERVE
Thaw at room temperature for 3 hours to serve cold with cream. Reheat in a moderate oven, 180°C/350°F/Gas 4, for 35 minutes to serve hot.
HIGH QUALITY STORAGE LIFE   4 months

Rich Cider Cake

300ml/½ pint cider
50g/2 oz dried apricots
50g/2 oz stoned dates
25g/1 oz stoned prunes
225g/8 oz butter
225g/8 oz dark soft brown
    sugar
3 eggs
275g/10 oz plain flour
salt
175g/6 oz currants
175g/6 oz sultanas
50g/2 oz raisins
50g/2 oz chopped peel
50g/2 oz chopped walnuts
50g/2 oz glacé cherries

TOPPING
150ml/¼ pint cider
50g/2 oz dried apricots
50g/2 oz glacé cherries
15g/½ oz sultanas
25g/1 oz walnut halves
15g/½ oz strips candied
    peel
40g/1½ oz Demerara sugar

Put the cider, chopped apricots, dates and prunes into a container, cover with a lid and soak overnight.

Cream the butter and sugar until light and fluffy, then beat in the eggs, one at a time. Add the sifted flour and salt with the currants, sultanas, raisins, peel, nuts and cherries, and fold lightly into the creamed mixture. Fold in the soaked fruit and any remaining liquid. Transfer to a greased and lined cake tin, make a deep hollow in the centre and bake in a very cool oven, 140°C/275°F/Gas 1, for 4 hours.

To make the topping, mix the cider, chopped apricots, cherries and sultanas overnight, and, when the cake goes into the oven, add the walnuts and peel. When the cake has cooked for 4 hours, drain the fruit for the topping, mix in the Demerara sugar and spread on top of the cake. Return to the oven for a further 30 minutes, then turn to 190°C/375°F/Gas 5 for 15 minutes. Lift out carefully and cool on a wire rack. Open freeze, then wrap in foil or polythene to store.

TO SERVE
Thaw at room temperature for 3 hours.
HIGH QUALITY STORAGE LIFE   2 months

Orange Frost Cake

125g/4 oz butter
50g/2 oz caster sugar
30ml/2 tablespoons clear
    honey
grated rind of ½ orange
2 eggs
150g/5 oz self-raising flour
30ml/2 tablespoons orange
    juice

ICING
125g/4 oz butter
175g/6 oz icing sugar
15ml/1 tablespoon clear
    honey
15ml/1 tablespoon hot
    water
orange colouring

FOR SERVING
mimosa balls *or* crystallized
    orange slices

Cream the butter and sugar together until light and fluffy. Beat in the honey and orange rind and add the eggs gradually. Fold in the flour, then add the orange juice and mix to a soft dropping consistency. Put into a greased and lined round sandwich tin. Bake in a fairly hot oven, 190°C/375°F/Gas 5, for 25 minutes. Turn out and cool on a wire rack.

To make the icing, soften the butter and beat in the sifted icing sugar. Beat in the honey and water, and a few drops of orange colouring if liked. Beat until creamy and smooth and spread on the cake, making soft peaks with the back of a teaspoon. Open freeze and then wrap in foil or polythene to store.

TO SERVE
Unwrap and thaw at room temperature for 3 hours. Decorate with mimosa balls or crystallized orange slices.
HIGH QUALITY STORAGE LIFE   4 months

Family Fruit Cake

225g/8 oz self-raising flour
1.25ml/¼ teaspoon salt
125g/4 oz butter
125g/4 oz soft brown sugar
125g/4 oz sultanas and
    raisins
50g/2 oz chopped mixed
    peel
grated rind of ½ lemon
1 egg
75ml/3 fl oz milk

Sift the flour and salt and rub in the butter until the mixture looks like fine breadcrumbs. Stir in the sugar, dried fruit, peel and grated rind, and mix lightly with the beaten egg and milk. Put into a greased and lined cake tin and bake in a moderate oven, 180°C/350°F/Gas 4, for 1½ hours. Cool on a wire rack. Wrap in polythene to freeze.

TO SERVE
Thaw in wrapping at room temperature for 3 hours.
HIGH QUALITY STORAGE LIFE   4 months

Marmalade Cake

175g/6 oz butter
175g/6 oz caster sugar
3 eggs
275g/10 oz self-raising flour
45ml/3 tablespoons chunky
    marmalade
50g/2 oz chopped mixed
    peel
grated rind of 1 orange
75ml/3 fl oz water

Beat the butter and sugar together until light and creamy. Beat in the egg yolks, one at a time, then 15ml/1 tablespoon of the flour. Stir in the marmalade, peel, orange rind and water, and fold in the remaining flour. Whisk the egg whites to soft peaks and fold into the cake mixture. Turn into a greased and lined cake tin and bake in a moderate oven, 180°C/350°F/Gas 4, for 1¼ hours. Cool on a wire rack and wrap in polythene to freeze.

TO SERVE
Thaw in wrappings at room temperature for 3 hours.
HIGH QUALITY STORAGE LIFE   4 months

Pineapple Upside-down Cake

1 medium pineapple
150g/5 oz butter
175g/6 oz brown sugar
8–10 glacé cherries
125g/4 oz caster sugar
1 egg
175g/6 oz plain flour
5ml/1 teaspoon baking
    powder
2.5ml/½ teaspoon salt
50ml/2 fl oz milk

Peel the pineapple and cut the flesh into rings. Melt 75g/3 oz butter and stir in the brown sugar until it melts. Pour this into a foil freezer container. Arrange the pineapple rings close together in the sugar and place a cherry in the centre of each ring. Cream the remaining butter with the caster sugar, beat in the egg, flour, baking powder and salt, and mix with the milk. Pour on to the pineapple and bake in a moderate oven, 180°C/350°F/Gas 4, for 40 minutes. Cool, cover and freeze.

TO SERVE
Heat in a moderate oven, 180°C/350°F/Gas 4, for 35 minutes, then turn out on to a hot plate and serve with cream.
HIGH QUALITY STORAGE LIFE   2 months

Pineapple Upside-down Cake

Yoghurt Cake

125g/4 oz butter
175g/6 oz caster sugar
grated rind of 1 lemon
3 eggs
175g/6 oz self-raising flour
175g/6 oz natural yoghurt
chopped peel

FOR SERVING
lemon water icing

Cream the butter and sugar, add the lemon rind and beat well. Add the egg yolks one at a time and beat in. Add the sifted flour alternately with the yoghurt and stir in the peel. Whisk the egg whites until stiff and fold into the mixture. Spoon into a greased loaf tin and bake at 180°C/350°F/Gas 4 for 1 hour. Turn out on to a wire rack and cool. Wrap in foil or polythene and freeze.

TO SERVE
Thaw at room temperature for 3 hours, and top with lemon water icing.
HIGH QUALITY STORAGE LIFE   4 months

Drop Scones

225g/8 oz plain flour
1.25ml/¼ teaspoon salt
2.5ml/½ teaspoon
   bicarbonate of soda
5ml/1 teaspoon cream of
   tartar
25g/1 oz sugar
1 egg
300ml/½ pint milk

Sift together the flour, salt, soda and cream of tartar. Stir in the sugar and mix to a batter with the egg and milk. Cook in spoonfuls on a lightly greased griddle or frying pan. When bubbles appear on the surface, turn and cook the other side. Cool in a cloth to keep soft. Pack in a rigid container with clingfilm between the layers, or pack in a polythene bag to freeze.

TO SERVE
Thaw at room temperature for 1 hour and spread with butter.
HIGH QUALITY STORAGE LIFE   2 months

Walnut Brownies

175g/6 oz margarine
25g/1 oz cocoa
175g/6 oz caster sugar
2 eggs
50g/2 oz plain flour
50g/2 oz chopped walnuts

FOR SERVING
caster sugar *or* melted plain
   chocolate

Melt 50g/2 oz margarine and stir in the cocoa. Set aside to cool. Cream the remaining margarine with the sugar until soft and gradually beat in the eggs. Fold in the sifted flour and add the chopped walnuts and the cocoa mixture. Put into a greased and base-lined tin and bake in a moderate oven, 180°C/350°F/Gas 4, for 45 minutes. Cool and turn out. Wrap in foil or polythene to freeze.

TO SERVE
Thaw at room temperature for 3 hours and sprinkle with caster sugar, or cover with melted plain chocolate. Cut in squares.
HIGH QUALITY STORAGE LIFE   4 months

Danish Pastry Pinwheels

225g/8 oz strong white flour
2.5ml/½ teaspoon salt
50g/2 oz sugar
15g/½ oz fresh yeast *or*
8g/¼ oz dried yeast
150ml/¼ pint warm water
75g/3 oz butter
mixed dried fruit
beaten egg
water icing

Sift the flour and salt and mix in the sugar. Blend the fresh yeast in the warm water, or reconstitute the dried yeast as directed on the packet. Mix with the flour and sugar to a soft, slightly sticky dough, and leave to rise in a warm place until increased by one-third in volume. Form the butter into a rectangle and dust with flour. Flatten the dough with the hands and fold with the fat in the centre like a parcel. Roll and fold twice like puff pastry. Leave in a cold place for 20 minutes, then roll and fold twice more and leave for 20 minutes. Roll out to 1.25cm/½ inch thickness and sprinkle with dried fruit. Roll up like a Swiss roll and cut into 1.25cm/½ inch slices. Place on a baking sheet and brush with beaten egg. Bake in a fairly hot oven, 190°C/375°F/Gas 5, for 30 minutes. Cool on a wire rack. The pastries may be frozen un-iced or with a light water icing. Pack in foil trays with a foil lid, or in boxes, and freeze.

TO SERVE
Remove wrappings and thaw at room temperatue for 1 hour.
HIGH QUALITY STORAGE LIFE   2 months

Éclairs

150ml/¼ pint water
50g/2 oz lard
50g/2 oz plain flour
a pinch of salt
2 eggs

FOR SERVING
lightly sweetened whipped cream
chocolate *or* coffee glacé icing

Put the water and lard into a pan and bring to the boil. Tip in the flour and salt and draw the pan from the heat. Beat until smooth with a wooden spoon. Cook for 3 minutes, beating very thoroughly so that the mixture is smooth and is not sticking to the sides of the pan. Cool. Whisk the eggs together and add small quantities to the flour mixture. Beat well between each addition until the mixture is soft and firm but holds its shape – it may not be necessary to add all the egg. Pipe in finger-lengths on to baking sheets and bake in a hot oven, 220°C/425°F/Gas 7, for 30 minutes. Cool on a rack, making a small slit in each éclair, to allow any steam to escape. Pack in rigid containers to freeze.

TO SERVE
Thaw at room temperature for 1 hour. Put éclairs on to a baking sheet. Heat in a moderate oven, 180°C/350°F/Gas 4, for 5 minutes. Cool and fill with lightly sweetened whipped cream. Top with chocolate or coffee glacé icing.
HIGH QUALITY STORAGE LIFE   1 month

Ring Doughnuts

225g/8 oz strong white
  flour
5ml/1 teaspoon salt
10ml/2 teaspoons sugar
15g/½ oz fresh yeast *or*
  8g/¼ oz dried yeast
150ml/¼ pint warm milk
15g/½ oz margarine

FOR SERVING
caster sugar

Sift the flour and salt and mix in the sugar. Blend the yeast in half the warm milk, or reconstitute the dried yeast as directed on the packet. Add the margarine to the remaining milk and cool until lukewarm. Mix the yeast liquid, milk and margarine into the flour, and knead well. Cover and leave in a warm place for 1 hour. Knead lightly and then roll out to 2.5cm/1 inch thick. Cut out 7.5cm/3 inch circles and then cut out centres with a 2.5cm/1 inch cutter. Roll out the cut-out centres and cut into extra rings as before. Put on baking trays and leave in a warm place for 20 minutes to rise. Fry 2 or 3 at a time in hot oil until golden-brown, then drain very well on kitchen paper. Cool and pack in polythene bags to freeze.

TO SERVE
Heat straight from the freezer in a fairly hot oven, 200°C/400°F/Gas 6, for 8 minutes. Roll in caster sugar and serve at once.
HIGH QUALITY STORAGE LIFE   1 month

Easter Biscuits

225g/8 oz plain flour
a pinch of salt
2.5ml/½ teaspoon mixed
  spice
75g/3 oz butter *or*
  margarine
75g/3 oz caster sugar
1 small beaten egg
75g/3 oz currants
milk

Sift the flour, salt and spice. Cream the fat and sugar until light and fluffy. Beat in a little egg and flour, then stir in the currants and remaining flour, adding a little more egg if necessary to make a firm paste. Roll out thinly, cut into large rounds and put on a greased tray. Prick with a fork, brush over with milk and sprinkle with caster sugar. Bake in a warm oven, 160°C/325°F/Gas 3, for 20 minutes. Cool on a rack. Pack in a rigid container with clingfilm between the layers, and freeze.

TO SERVE
Thaw at room temperature for 1 hour.
HIGH QUALITY STORAGE LIFE   2 months

Easter Biscuits

Waffles

125g/4 oz self-raising flour
a pinch of salt
15ml/1 tablespoon caster
  sugar
1 egg
30ml/2 tablespoons melted
  butter
150ml/¼ pint milk

Mix together the dry ingredients in a bowl. Add the egg yolk, melted butter and milk, and beat well to a smooth batter. Whisk the egg white stiffly and fold into the batter.

Pour enough batter into the waffle iron to run over the surface. Do not overfill or the mixture will spill, and the waffle will not be able to rise properly. Close the iron over the mixture and leave to cook for 2–3 minutes, turning once. Waffles for freezing should not be over-brown. Leave to cool, and pack in foil or polythene to freeze.

TO SERVE
Heat frozen under a grill or in a hot oven. Serve with a choice of maple syrup (the traditional accompaniment), golden syrup or melted butter; or sandwich with layers of jam, whipped cream and redcurrant jelly, and dredge with icing sugar.
HIGH QUALITY STORAGE LIFE   2 months

Coffee Kisses

175g/6 oz self-raising flour
a pinch of salt
75g/3 oz butter *or*
  margarine
50g/2 oz caster sugar
1 egg yolk
5ml/1 teaspoon coffee
  essence

ICING
50g/2 oz butter
75g/3 oz icing sugar
5ml/1 teaspoon coffee
  essence

Sift the flour and salt, rub in the butter or margarine, and stir in the sugar. Mix to a stiff paste with the egg yolk and coffee essence. Shape into 24 small balls and put on a greased baking tray. Bake in a fairly hot oven, 190°C/375°F/Gas 5, for 15 minutes. Cool on a rack.

Mix the icing by gradually beating together the butter, icing sugar and coffee essence until soft and fluffy. Sandwich the 'kisses' together in pairs with the icing. Pack in a rigid container with clingfilm between the layers, and freeze.

TO SERVE
Thaw at room temperature for 1 hour, and dust with icing sugar.
HIGH QUALITY STORAGE LIFE   2 months

Marshmallow Biscuits

40g/1½ oz butter
225g/8 oz marshmallows
125g/4 oz plain chocolate
125g/4 oz rice krispies
  cereal

Put the butter into a bowl over hot water, or into the top of a double saucepan. Melt and stir in the marshmallows and broken chocolate. Stir until smooth and creamy. Put the cereal into a bowl and stir in the chocolate mixture. Put into a greased tin about 2.5cm/1 inch thick. Leave for about 1 hour until cold and firm. Cut into squares and pack in a rigid container to freeze.

TO SERVE
Thaw at room temperature for 2 hours.
HIGH QUALITY STORAGE LIFE   2 months

INDEX

Page references to instructions on freezing individual ingredients are in **bold** type.

All recipe entries are in italic, eg *Ratatouille 94*